Business Communication
Pocket Guide

Writing for Business

Professionalism, Integrity &
Power

Ellen Jovin

NICHOLAS   BREALEY
PUBLISHING

BOSTON • LONDON

This edition published in 2019 by Nicholas Brealey Publishing
An imprint of John Murray Press

An Hachette UK company

23 22 21 20 19   1 2 3 4 5 6 7 8 9 10

A CIP catalogue record for this title is available from the British
Library

A catalogue record for this book is available from the
Library of Congress.

ISBN 978-1-529-30345-2
US eBook ISBN 978-1-529-30354-4
UK eBook ISBN 978-1-529-30347-6

Printed and bound in the United States of America.

John Murray Press policy is to use papers that are natural, renewable,
and recyclable products and made from wood grown in sustainable
forests. The logging and manufacturing processes are expected to
conform to the environmental regulations of the country of origin.

John Murray Press Ltd   Nicholas Brealey Publishing
Carmelite House   Hachette Book Group
50 Victoria Embankment   53 State Street
London EC4Y 0DZ   Boston, MA 02109, USA
Tel: 020 3122 6000   Tel: (617) 263 1834

www.nbuspublishing.com

Contents

Introduction

A Philosophy of Workplace Writing

Businesspeople sometimes write as if they are being paid by the pound for their words. If you added up all the pages, including email, written each year at US businesses, perhaps a good half of the material could be cut with no loss whatsoever—but with a whole lot of benefit to the writers' goals and the readers' well-being.

The strange thing is, no matter how much people hate reading unnecessarily long, unnecessarily complex business documents, many continue to write them. Writing for business is practical in nature. Writing should help people achieve their practical goals, not work in opposition to them. It is time to smash several common misconceptions about what makes good business writing good.

First, unnecessary complexity in business writing is a weakness, not a strength. Don't admire a piece of writing simply because it sounds important or because you can't figure out what the person is trying to say. Some ideas are complex. Many are not. If you create extra labor for the reader because you are making a straightforward idea hard to understand, you are doing it wrong. Treasure simplicity.

Second, spinning is bad. Do not spin the facts. Manipulative writing violates the trust of the reader, and there is no good writing without trust. The best business writing presents truth, even unpleasant truth, straightforwardly and with grace.

People dissemble in various ways. They may omit facts, or use vague, deceptive language to obscure the truth, or wait five paragraphs to tell the big and critical bad news because they want to talk about trivial positive or neutral details first. If you have failed to meet an important deadline, don't stash it in the final paragraph of your email about that project. If you are ending a tuition reimbursement program, don't present it in a falsely chipper tone. If you are firing people, don't hide behind impenetrable euphemisms.

Third, there is not one single magical and elusive way people are supposed to write, just hovering out there, if only you could grab it. There is variety in professional writing in the world. Different people have different voices. Yes, there are features workplace writing should have—and also shouldn't have—and this book examines them in some detail. But don't look at the people next to you and automatically think they are closer to the correct style than you are because they sound fancier. Admire the writing that slides easily into your head, not the writing that hurts it.

Fourth, it is generally untrue that there should be an enormous gap between formal and informal writing. At work there usually isn't that big a gap if you are doing it right. So much of business writing today is email, where you are writing in first person (*I*) to someone you are addressing in second person (*you*). Even in your least formal email, you shouldn't be writing as though you are texting your best friend since elementary school. In your most formal correspondence, you should still sound like the person you are, not a business robot speaking in some official business-robot voice.

Business writing isn't separate from us as people. Yes, it involves writing about work—but it is nonetheless writing by people, for people. What do you want as a human being? You want people to respect your time, give you good information, help you do your job better, be attuned to your needs and interests. You would presumably prefer that they be nice to you than not. Surely you would prefer that they talk to you like a person, not a robot.

Since the majority of business writing for most working professionals now consists of email, this book spends a significant amount of time on email details and examples throughout the first half of the book. But in the second half, it also explicitly covers numerous other document types—letters, memos, reports, proposals, and more. The writing principles throughout the book, even in the email section, tend to apply broadly to multiple written forms you will encounter at work.

For all writing types, your readers will respect truthfulness. They will respect you for having an authentic voice. They will respect you for being real. Integrity, authenticity, truthfulness are at the heart of effective workplace communication—and at the heart of a rewarding professional and personal life.

Ellen L. Jovin

Chapter 1

Getting to the Point
in Email

I n email, you have two opportunities to get to the point quickly: (1) in the subject line and (2) your main idea, equivalent to the idea of the thesis you may remember from when you were in school— that one sentence in the opening that summed up the point of the whole paper.

Short or long, in most email messages, you should skip a line after your salutation, between paragraphs, and before your closing (e.g., *Regards*). You do not need to indent. The email below illustrates appropriate spacing.

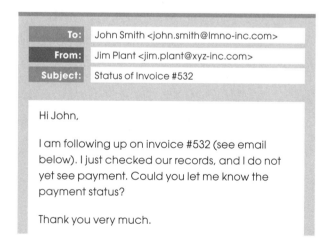

To:	John Smith <john.smith@lmno-inc.com>
From:	Jim Plant <jim.plant@xyz-inc.com>
Subject:	Status of Invoice #532

Hi John,

I am following up on invoice #532 (see email below). I just checked our records, and I do not yet see payment. Could you let me know the payment status?

Thank you very much.

Regards,
Jim

Jim Plant
Director, Marketing | XYZ, Inc.
123 Anywhere Street, New York, NY 10024
jim.plant@xyz-inc.com | xyz-inc.com
(212) 555-6789

Sample Email Format

A note: from this point on, the signature block (i.e., the contact information you see at the bottom) will be excluded from email examples unless the discussion addresses that part of the email specifically. That does *not* mean you should exclude them from email, because you usually shouldn't!

1.1 Email Subject Lines

The subject line of an email needs to be brief yet descriptive. It is by scanning subject lines that many people can find your message among a slew of other incoming messages competing for their attention.

Below are examples of bad and good subject lines with commentary on each.

Bad Subject Lines	
Example	*Commentary*
Meeting	Unhelpful when reader is trying to decide whether this email is something that needs immediate attention. Useless when someone is searching for it even a day later.
technology report	Too vague. Lack of capitalization looks careless and unprofessional.
Report on technology expenses for the third quarter of 2019 attached	Too long. Might get truncated on the screen. Syntax is convoluted.
I'm not sure where the meeting is can you send me the address?	Don't write your email in the subject line. Also, don't write run-ons in subject lines (or anywhere else).
Language proposals	Too vague. Proposals for what event? Are the proposals being submitted with this email, or is this a request for proposals?
(Empty subject line)	Subject-free emails tend to look like spam, and the lack of information is annoying to recipients. Seems lazy.

Good Subject Lines	
Example	*Commentary*
1/13/20 Schedule for Cleveland Marketing Meeting	Professional capitalization. Specific information with date. Good length. Specifies the aspect of meeting being discussed.
Technology Expense Report Q3 2019	Information presented compactly and in a way that is easy to process.
Language Enthusiast Conference 2021: Call for Presentation Proposals	Uses a colon effectively to break up information and make it more readable. Precise language.

For capitalization of your subject line, you have two main options:

- Capitalize the subject line as you would a title, beginning everything except minor words with capital letters.
- Capitalize the first word of the subject, as well as any proper nouns, but begin all or most other words with lowercase letters. This makes sense especially if your subject line is closer to a short sentence than a simple noun phrase.

The decision is a stylistic and aesthetic one, based on your own preferences and the context.

In managing an ongoing dialogue, it can sometimes be helpful to change subject lines to reflect evolving subject matter. Alternatively, begin a new dialogue.

1.2 The Subject Is Not Part of Your Email Message

Most email messages are no longer than a few paragraphs, and many messages are much shorter—a few lines. There is no minimum length requirement. The ideal length is this: as long as you need to get your point across.

No matter the length of the email, the subject line is not a substitute for a main idea in the email itself. People who write their emails as though the subject line is part of the message often confuse their readers. Here is an example of such an email:

To:	Ali Gold <ali.gold@lmno-inc.com>
From:	Jim Plant <jim.plant@xyz-inc.com>
Subject:	Proposal is now with the client…

…so let's start on the next one this afternoon, okay?

Confusing Use of Subject Line

If the reader starts reading in the freeform box, as many people do, without first looking at the subject line, the email will make no sense. It's easy to make your emails more readable. Just do it!

Here's a solution for this one:

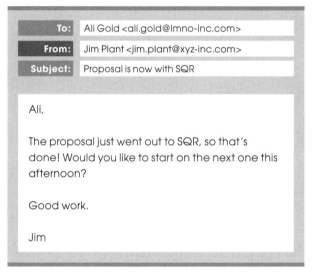

To:	Ali Gold <ali.gold@lmno-inc.com>
From:	Jim Plant <jim.plant@xyz-inc.com>
Subject:	Proposal is now with SQR

Ali,

The proposal just went out to SQR, so that's done! Would you like to start on the next one this afternoon?

Good work.

Jim

Revised Email and Subject Line

This next sample email shows a different misuse of the subject line. If the reader, Ali, skips the subject line, she won't know what the writer, Jim, is talking about, because he doesn't mention the topic of the email in the message itself. The email needs to have standalone integrity without the subject line.

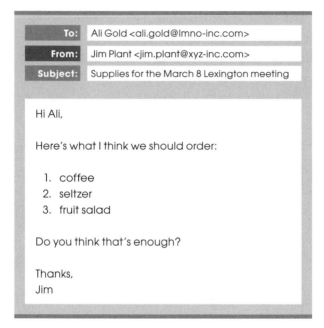

To: | Ali Gold <ali.gold@lmno-inc.com>

From: | Jim Plant <jim.plant@xyz-inc.com>

Subject: | Supplies for the March 8 Lexington meeting

Hi Ali,

Here's what I think we should order:

1. coffee
2. seltzer
3. fruit salad

Do you think that's enough?

Thanks,
Jim

Confusing Use of Subject Line #2

You personally may read every email's subject line. But many people start in the box where the freeform email is composed. The following revision shows how to mention the topic twice, once in the subject and once in the email opening, in a way that isn't boringly repetitive.

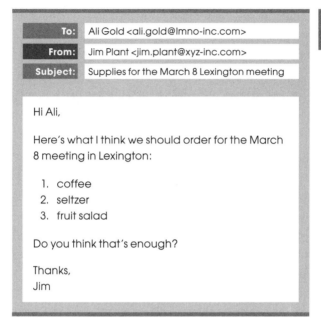

To: Ali Gold <ali.gold@lmno-inc.com>

From: Jim Plant <jim.plant@xyz-inc.com>

Subject: Supplies for the March 8 Lexington meeting

Hi Ali,

Here's what I think we should order for the March 8 meeting in Lexington:

1. coffee
2. seltzer
3. fruit salad

Do you think that's enough?

Thanks,
Jim

Successful Integration of Subject into Email

1.3 The Point of Your Email

Somewhere within the first paragraph of your email, the reader needs to understand your purpose. Are you responding to a previous message from the recipient? Do you need a particular file? Are you trying to set up a meeting? Do you want to convince your manager that you need a new piece of software?

Whether your email message is two sentences or six paragraphs in length, you should state the main point of your message as soon as possible. In short emails, it is possible to send a perfectly sound email just one sentence in length, as long as that sentence clearly expresses your purpose.

Let's take an example. Imagine that you are writing an email to your manager, Deanna. You have researched some new technology, and you have concluded that spending $10,000 on new hardware and software will save your department about $40,000 per quarter in tech-support costs. You have written and are attaching a three-page proposal describing the new technology and explaining the cost reductions.

Below is a common approach to this type of email.

To:	Deanna Smith <deanna.smith@xyz-inc.com>
From:	Marcia Rait <marcia.rait@xyz-inc.com>
Subject:	New Technology Purchases

Good morning, Deanna.

I have attached a three-page proposal I wrote describing $10,000 in new technology I am recommending our department purchase. The technology consists of new hardware and software.

I believe it would save us approximately $40,000 per quarter in support costs.

I would be glad to discuss this idea with you in more detail.

Thank you,
Marcia

Chronological Order: Spending First

Now, imagine a fire alarm goes off in the building right after Deanna finishes reading the subject, "New Technology Purchases," and the first sentence, "I have attached a three-page proposal I wrote describing $10,000 in new technology I am recommending our department purchase." That is what Deanna now has in her head as she descends the stairs and then stands out on the street in a snowstorm, waiting for the fire department to okay reentry. All she knows as the snow swirls around her head and the heavy wind keeps unwrapping her scarf is that Marcia wants something from her—and that it will cost her money.

That's a shame, because the only reason Marcia is writing this email is that she wants to save Deanna, the department, and the company money. However, Deanna has no way to know that until she gets back inside from the snowstorm and finishes reading the email. Good weather or bad, why make her wait several sentences to be happy to receive the email?

The following revision solves this problem by putting the main idea—the savings—in the first sentence. The subject line, "Technology Cost-Savings Proposal," does the same.

To:	Deanna Smith <deanna.smith@xyz-inc.com>
From:	Marcia Rait <marcia.rait@xyz-inc.com>
Subject:	Technology Cost-Savings Proposal

Good morning, Deanna.

I have attached a brief proposal I wrote describing a way we could dramatically reduce our technology costs.

Although this idea would require a onetime investment of $10,000 in new hardware and software, the new technology would save us approximately $40,000 per quarter in support costs.

I would be glad to discuss this idea with you in more detail.

Thank you,
Marcia

Most Important Idea First

Now Deanna will be happy as soon as she starts reading. The approach used in the revised email makes it more likely that Deanna will say yes. The department will save money, Deanna will forward the email so that other departments can save money, the firm will save a lot of money, and the writer will get a promotion and a raise!

Think big. Why not?

1

Chapter 2

Email Salutations

An incomprehensibly large amount of email travels around the world each day. Often it is email that has been composed at high speed. High-speed or not, work email still needs to be professional. It should generally include appropriate salutations and closings, signature files, and standard punctuation and capitalization. This chapter focuses on salutations: how you greet the recipient(s).

Although recipient information appears in the To field, for most professional emails you should still greet the person in the message itself. A greeting adds warmth that a name plopped into the To field does not.

The choices you make should suit you, suit your recipient, and suit the context.

Salutations for business letters are limited and therefore easy:

Dear Ms. Gregg:
Dear Ramona:

No such luck with email. It's complicated.

Salutation culture varies significantly from one organization to the next. Employees of a museum may well have different salutation habits than employees of a large bank in the same city. Small firms with older employees are likely to have different habits than a high-tech company whose employees are mostly under 30 and wear jeans to work. Whatever you read in these pages, pay attention to your own culture—and the cultures you communicate with—and use common sense to determine what will work best for you.

2.1 Salutation Punctuation

Before we discuss the wording of salutations, a note on punctuation: you will not find a universal accepted standard for punctuating email greetings. People have individual tastes and preferences. For some people who grew up with strict grammar classes, having no comma before the name *Mary* in these greetings would be untenable:

> Hi Mary,
> Hello Mary,
> Good morning Mary,

They prefer to put a comma between the greeting and the name, like this:

Hi, Mary,
Hello, Mary,
Good morning, Mary,

The argument for the comma before the name is that each of these examples contains instances of direct address. In other words, you have an utterance, then you address the person, so it needs a comma. But having two commas together like that is unacceptable to many, so a punctuation battle then ensues over how to end the salutation.

Hello, Mary,
Hello, Mary –
Hello, Mary.
Hello, Mary!
Hello, Mary:

There is not an absolute rule about what is most acceptable. The period strikes some younger members of the workforce as unfriendly. It is hard to please everyone all the time, which is why email is so challenging yet also so full of interesting opportunities to tailor your approach to your audience.

This is where the concept of mirroring comes in handy. If you are writing to a client or manager, consider what they do as you make your own choices.

2.2 Email Salutations for One Recipient

Listed below are various salutations seen in email messages to one recipient, with commentary on each. They are organized roughly from most formal to least formal.

*   *   *

Dear Mr. Smith:
Dear Robin:

These two formal salutations are letter-like. Use of them is waning in the United States as memories of business letters fade, but they are still helpful when you are emailing a person you do not really know—for example, a prospective client. You could use *Dear* with a surname when writing to someone who is much older than you are, someone you would like to convince to donate to your nonprofit, a potential employer you hope will hire you, people who work in other countries, and so on. Using *Dear* with the first name is naturally less formal, but still more formal than many other greetings.

Increasingly, younger people complain that *Dear* sounds weird—like something for a letter to Mom or a boyfriend—but the salutation *Dear* persists in formal circles, academic circles, and international correspondence. It still has a legitimate place in your email repertoire.

*   *   *

> Robin,
> Robin –

The recipient's name by itself is fine as a salutation in many contexts. It can sound abrupt to some people, but it is a solid, professional opening for many types of email messages. If clients and managers use this with you, consider using it with them. Above all, do not assume people mean it rudely when they address you this way. Often people—especially people on the older end of the workforce—just happen to find the name alone more professional than using *Hi*. If your email begins with the recipient's name followed by "I really enjoyed your presentation yesterday," it is highly unlikely the reader will object.

*   *   *

> Good morning, Robin.
> Good morning, Robin –
> Good morning Robin,
> Good morning, Robin:
> Good morning, Robin!

This salutation, which you will find punctuated in a variety of ways, only some of which are shown here, can be a useful way to begin email messages, because it is simultaneously formal and friendly. Of course, at the time you send the message, it should actually be morning in the recipient's time zone. It doesn't really matter what time it is where you are, nor does it much matter whether they are likely to read the email when it is still their morning. Do not capitalize the *m* in *morning*.

*   *   *

2

Good afternoon, Robin.
Good afternoon, Robin –
Good afternoon Robin,
Good afternoon, Robin:
Good afternoon, Robin!

Good afternoon feels more formal than *Good morning*. That is because people don't tend to say it much in their daily lives. Maybe it is also in part because it has so many syllables. It can still be helpful when you are emailing in the afternoon, however, and are in need of a professional greeting.

*   *   *

Hello Robin,
Hello, Robin –
Hello, Robin:
Hello, Robin.
Hello, Robin!
Hello, Robin,

This salutation is used a lot in email. The first option, with one comma, is perhaps the most common. However, for people who were taught to use a comma between *Hello* and the recipient's name, there are a number of alternatives, listed here. Each option has its own advocates and opponents. *Hello* is favored by some over *Hi* because it is less casual.

*   *   *

Hi Robin,
Hi, Robin –
Hi, Robin,
Hi, Robin.
Hi, Robin!

The first *Hi* greeting shown here, with one comma, is common these days. Some people still put a comma before the name, for reasons described in 2.1. Apart from punctuation, be careful about using *Hi* in formal contexts. Some organizations are more formal than others. If you are writing to someone to whom you provide service and that person never, ever writes *Hi* in email to you, consider carefully whether you should use it yourself.

*   *   *

Hey Robin,

Friendly greetings between colleagues can promote collegiality, but be careful about how often you use them. Many people dislike *Hey* and find it unsuitable for work. Emails get forwarded—do you want your *Hey* to make the rounds?

2.3 Email Salutations for an Unknown Recipient

Sometimes you don't know the recipient's name—for instance, when you are writing to generic email addresses (beginning with info@, hr@, customerservice@, etc.). This section discusses salutations for anonymous situations.

* * *

2

> To Whom It May Concern:
>
> Dear Sir or Madam:

Although these two formulations sound old-fashioned and stuffy to some, they have been around for a long time in business correspondence. You can use them in cases such as an emailed inquiry regarding a request for information or an emailed complaint. If you don't like them, or if you would like to be more inclusive than the second one allows, you have numerous options below.

* * *

> Greetings.   Good afternoon.
> Greetings –   Good afternoon –
> Greetings,   Good afternoon,
> Greetings: Good afternoon:
> Greetings!   Good afternoon!
> Good morning.   Hello.
> Good morning –   Hello –
> Good morning,   Hello,
> Good morning: Hello:
> Good morning!   Hello!

Hello is the least formal on the preceding list. As you can see, there are not only numerous wording options but also numerous punctuation options. All are in use, and all are acceptable—at least to some people. You can't please everyone all the time, but the reality is, most people don't pay that much attention. That doesn't mean *you* shouldn't pay attention!

2.4 Email Salutations for Multiple Recipients

Addressing a group of people through email can pose a formidable challenge. Many of the most popular ones—*Hi all!*—sound a bit unnatural even to some of their users.

To formulate a salutation for multiple people, consider the composition of the group you will be addressing. If you are writing to your co-workers in the marketing department, for example, you could perhaps begin your message with one of the following salutations:

Dear Colleagues:
Dear Marketing Colleagues:

The appropriateness of these salutations, however, would depend on contextual details. Below are comments on various salutations, some good and some not so good, that appear in group email messages. They are, once again, generally listed from most formal to least formal.

2

*   *   *

> Dear Sirs:
> Dear Gentlemen:

Don't use these anymore. In a working world populated by both women and men, these salutations are out of date. Theoretically they could still be used in a context where every recipient was male, but even in those cases, the formulations are likely to come across as old-fashioned. *Gentlemen* is old-fashioned, *Sirs* is old-fashioned, and so is assuming everyone is male. Even if the initial group is all male, emails containing such openings can and frequently do raise eyebrows when they are forwarded.

*   *   *

> Dear Colleagues:
> Dear Colleagues,
> Hello, Colleagues:
> Hello Colleagues,
> Hello, Colleagues!

These salutations can be used to address the people in your department or division, assuming that you are not junior to the people you are addressing as your colleagues. You should be senior to or have the same level of seniority as the email recipients. The greetings are respectful and, well, collegial. Some people will gripe about the *Dear*, so included here are three non-*Dear* options. You can't please everyone all the time, but it's nice to get closer rather than farther from that goal.

*   *   *

> Dear Team:
> Dear Team,
> Team,
> Team –
> Hello, Team:
> Hello Team,
> Hi Team,

This set of salutations is similar to the ones above for colleagues. These are sometimes used with a team working together as a unit within a department or maybe across corporate divisions on a particular project. As with greetings referring to colleagues, it's probably a good idea to avoid these unless you have the same seniority as the people you are addressing or are senior to them.

*   *   *

> Good morning, everyone.
>
> Greetings –
>
> Hello, everyone!

You can try various permutations of these salutations, using punctuation options shown in earlier examples. If you dislike ending with a period, as shown in the first example, there are always other options, such as an exclamation point (for pep) or a dash instead.

* * *

Jane and Tim,

Hi, Jane and Tim!

Good morning,
Jane and Tim:

If you are addressing two people, you may use their names in combination with various greetings for individual recipients discussed in 2.2. Some common options appear here. For emails going to more than two people, it can sound awkward to refer to all of them by name. Three names is probably the maximum that will sound natural, and if each name has, say, four syllables, you may need to give up earlier!

* * *

Hello all,
Hi all,

Quite a few people use these two greetings while nonetheless finding them awkward and unsatisfactory. *Hi all* in particular sounds like you are arriving at, say, a barbecue. (Maybe one day when email culture has matured further, we will stop using salutations in emails sent to groups, because group greetings sometimes sound pretty unnatural. However, we're not there yet.) Be careful about using these two salutations in more formal work environments. Observe what others do first, and proceed with caution.

*   *   *

> Gentlemen,
> Ladies,
> Guys,

These are increasingly poor choices for the workplace. Even if you are writing to an all-male or all-female group, email gets forwarded, and the terms *ladies* and *gentlemen* are often associated with old-fashioned notions of femininity and masculinity rather than mere gender. Many people dislike being referred to this way. Lastly, even if you use and understand *guys* in a gender-neutral way, not everyone does.

*   *   *

> No greeting
> whatsoever

Many people don't like to receive emails without salutations. Nonetheless, if your corporate culture supports it, sending a mass email with no greeting at all can make sense. Such an email is, after all, virtually identical in form to the traditional print memo, which did not contain any greeting at all.

2.5 Recipient Names in Email

It is terrible etiquette to get people's names wrong, so let's discuss how a simple thing like a name can go awry. This discussion is relevant not only for email but also for business letters and, well, general existence.

- **Shortened names and nicknames.** If a person's name happens to be one that is often shortened—*Michael*, for example—don't automatically assume that this particular individual is in the habit of shortening it. Use *Michael* unless you come across concrete evidence that the person uses *Mike*. That evidence may come from sources such as the bottom of an email—if he signs off as *Mike*—or maybe repeated voicemail messages from him starting off, "Hi, this is Mike."

  Once you learn that the recipient prefers the shortened form or some other nickname, use that version of the name. Store that information in your contact management software to remind yourself.

- **Spelling.** Triple-check unusual and unfamiliar names. If you successfully spell a name that is chronically misspelled, that can make a good impression.

- **Honorifics and gender.** The term *honorific* refers to the *Ms.*, *Dr.*, etc., before a person's name. It doesn't come up in business correspondence as much as it used to, but if you do write formally, use the honorific that the person prefers: *Dr.*, *Prof.*, *Ms.*, *Mr.*, and so on. If a woman specifically requests that you address her with *Mrs.* or *Miss*, naturally you should honor her request. The same goes for the gender-neutral *Mx*. If you don't know a person's preference and you feel the first name alone is too informal, then consider using the first and last names together. It sounds odd, but it is better than guessing at an honorific and getting it wrong.

Dear Drew Blake:

Do not lowercase recipients' names. The Shift key is so very close to you!

Just Don't

Hi rob,

2.6 May I Stop Greeting You Yet?

In ongoing dialogues, you may consider deleting the greeting after the initial exchange, but if you are writing to clients or to people at your firm who are senior to you—or anyone else to whom you provide service—do not delete the salutation until they begin doing so themselves.

Chapter 3

Email Closings

E mail closings provide fewer conundrums than email openings, but it is still impossible to come up with a one-size-fits-all solution. Heed your audience, your context, your own style, and other factors. This chapter includes commentary on various options currently in use.

3.1 Closing Format

The example below shows a sample closing, accompanied by a signature file (covered in detail in 3.3).

Regards,
Tim

Tim Jackson
Accounting Department
XYZ, Inc.
234 Any Street
Anytown, CA 94501
Work: (415) 555-1201
Cell: (415) 555-1892
timothy.jackson@xyz-inc.com
xyz-inc.com

Closing Format, Typical Email

His closing word—*Regards*—and name appear on consecutive lines.

Don't be troubled by the name repetition. The signature block is automatic; it's like wallpaper. Adding your name after the closing word or words is the equivalent of signing an old-fashioned letter, and it adds warmth and a sense of completeness to your email. Especially if you address someone by first name, you should close with your own first name.

Some people put periods after their names in closings. There is no need for a period after your name. Don't do it!

Incorrect

Regards,

Tim.

Correct

Regards,

Tim

As a general rule, don't sign off with initials unless you wish to be addressed that way.

3.2 Closing Words

Below are some common email closings, accompanied by comments on possible applications and beginning with the most formal.

*   *   *

Sincerely,
Susana Rojas

Sincerely is a polite, professional way to close. It is most appropriate for quite formal emails, such as initial communications with prospective clients or emails to donors to a nonprofit. It typically appears in formal email that is acting as a kind of business letter substitute.

*   *   *

Regards,
Susana

Regards has been a safe, acceptable closing term for a long time in many email situations, ranging from fairly casual to quite formal. It seems to have fewer fans, however, among younger emailers, who sometimes report finding it cold or unfriendly. *Regards* remains popular, but some people like to add adjectives.

*   *   *

Next we have the three adjectives often used to warm up a barebones *Regards*. Each has both detractors and

Best regards,
Susana

Kind regards,
Susana

Warm regards,
Susana

advocates. *Kind regards* is the most formal of the three, *Best regards* is almost surely the most common, and *Warm regards,* while polite and friendly, may strike some as too intimate or gushy. Know your environment! Picking a closing is an art, not a science.

*   *   *

Thank you,
Susana

This closing is ideal when you want to show appreciation for something the recipient has done or is going to do for you. Use it often, but not when there is no reason to be thanking people, because then it sounds as though you are on autopilot and not paying attention to what you are saying.

*   *   *

Thank you
very much.

Regards,
Susana

If you want to be very appreciative and say *Thank you very much,* then you can keep that as a separate sentence and add a different closing.

*   *   *

Best seems to be increasingly common as a closing, especially among people who dislike *Regards.* Despite

Best,
Susana

its popularity, plenty of recipients dislike it because it feels incomplete. What does it mean? Best wishes? Best regards? All the best? Best email ever? On the other hand, *Sincerely* never made much sense as a closing either, so prospects for *Best* seem solid.

*   *   *

Thanks,
Susana

This is more informal and less appreciative than *Thank you*. *Thanks* is appropriate if someone has done the email equivalent of handing you a soda. If you have reason to be more appreciative, *Thank you* is a better choice.

*   *   *

Susana

For quick, casual emails to people with whom you have an established business relationship, closing with just your first name is a common and acceptable practice. It's also fine for replies in ongoing email chains.

*   *   *

No closing
whatsoever

Email dialogues can go on for a while. At some point, it is often fine to stop including a greeting as well as a closing. If you are writing to a manager or a client, follow their lead and let them stop including these elements first, then go ahead and do it yourself.

3.3 Signature Files

The signature file, also known as a signature block or signature, is the block of information that tells people who you are and how to reach you. A simple signature file might look something like this:

Renée Jones
Director, Training
XYZ, Inc.
123 Anywhere Street
New York, NY 10024
(212) 555-0469
renee.jones@xyz-inc.com
xyz-inc.com

Sample Signature File #1

If you're not sure whether or not to include your signature file, include it. It helps an email appear polished and professional; it is like letterhead for email. If recipients of a message don't know you at all, the absence of a signature file is potentially irksome and reduces your chances of getting a response. Finally, you should (usually) make it as easy as possible for recipients to find you. By including contact information in your standard communications, you enable them to reach you with minimal effort.

If you work for an organization with a standard signature block template, use it. There are two things people often omit that can be helpful to include:

- **Email address.** Yes, your email address *is* in the From field, but if someone forwards your email, your email address may not appear in the forwarded chain.
- **Physical work address.** It is annoying to email recipients to have to ask for an emailer's address. People who need to meet with you or mail things to you will appreciate your including it in the signature. It is also kind of nice for an email recipient to know where the emailer is in the world. If you can't or don't want to include your address, that's okay, but do have a good reason for that choice

Think carefully before including social media. Don't include it if it overwhelms your other professional information, or if you are not 100% professional on social media. If you are at an organization, consider whether other people there include social media; if they don't, you probably shouldn't either.

If you include your cell number in your signature, be prepared to empty out your voicemail regularly. Full voicemail is frustrating. Including that information in your signature means you are committing to keeping your voicemail available.

Don't include favorite lines such as:

3

Have a blessed day.

Please consider the environment. Do you really need to print this email?

Many people either are not religious or may not share your religious beliefs. And there is no epidemic of people running around automatically printing their work email. Don't micromanage autonomous adults. They most likely won't print an email unless they need to, and if they do need to, being told not to could be annoying.

Avoid weird fonts, colors, rainbows, dancing penguins, etc., and proofread with punctiliousness! There is no such thing as overproofreading your contact details. Signature files have been espied with errors in the street address, phone number, and even email address.

Here is another sample signature format:

Marta Thomas | Director, Marketing
ZYX, Inc. | 345 Arthropod St. | New York, NY 10024
O (212) 555-0469 | M (646) 555-1472
marta.thomas@zyx-inc.com | zyx-inc.com

Sample Signature File #2

As you can see, it is significantly more compressed than the first example in this section.

If you don't work at a company with a standard signature format, look at the signature files in the emails you receive and purloin their best features for your own signature. Signature-file fashion evolves, and it's good to stay current.

If you are having an ongoing email dialogue with someone, you may want to omit the signature file in subsequent messages that accumulate within the same email chain. It isn't necessary to do so, but piles of signatures can make an email chain seem longer than it is.

Chapter 4

Email Models and
Makeovers

T his chapter is dedicated to email makeovers. Examples range from the judicious use of bulleting to attachment management to formality fixes.

4.1 Bullets Are Helpful But No Panacea!

Bulleting and numbered lists can help organize information so that it is easier to read. Compare the following two emails:

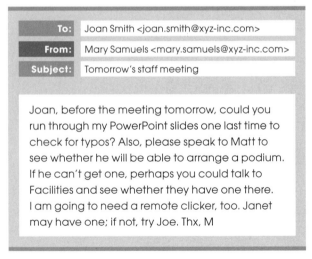

To:	Joan Smith <joan.smith@xyz-inc.com>
From:	Mary Samuels <mary.samuels@xyz-inc.com>
Subject:	Tomorrow's staff meeting

Joan, before the meeting tomorrow, could you run through my PowerPoint slides one last time to check for typos? Also, please speak to Matt to see whether he will be able to arrange a podium. If he can't get one, perhaps you could talk to Facilities and see whether they have one there. I am going to need a remote clicker, too. Janet may have one; if not, try Joe. Thx, M

List of Tasks in a Blob

To: Joan Smith <joan.smith@xyz-inc.com>

From: Mary Samuels <mary.samuels@xyz-inc.com>

Subject: Tomorrow's staff meeting

Joan,

Before the meeting tomorrow, could you please do the following:

1. Run through my PowerPoint slides one last time to check for typos.
2. Speak to Matt to see whether he will be able to arrange a podium. If he can't get one, perhaps you could talk to Facilities and see whether they have one there.
3. Get a remote clicker from Janet or Joe.

Thank you,
Mary

Revised Email with Tidily Numbered Tasks

The second, revised email has numbered tasks, making it much easier to read and therefore more likely to get the kind of organized, systematic response Mary would presumably like from Joan.

There is such a thing as too much bulleting, however. If you are creating monstrous, endless bulleted lists and going into syntactical and stylistic contortions to make everything parallel grammatically, cut back! Not everything in life needs to be bulleted. Here's an example where the writer went way overboard.

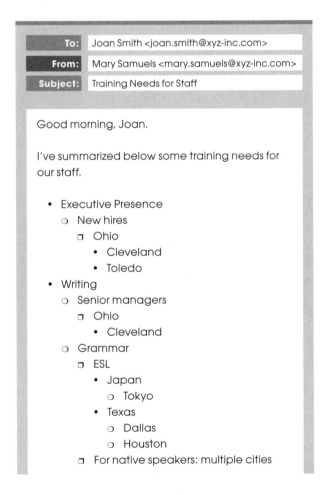

To: Joan Smith <joan.smith@xyz-inc.com>

From: Mary Samuels <mary.samuels@xyz-inc.com>

Subject: Training Needs for Staff

Good morning, Joan.

I've summarized below some training needs for our staff.

- Executive Presence
  - New hires
    - Ohio
      - Cleveland
      - Toledo
- Writing
  - Senior managers
    - Ohio
      - Cleveland
  - Grammar
    - ESL
      - Japan
        - Tokyo
      - Texas
        - Dallas
        - Houston
    - For native speakers: multiple cities

- Spreadsheet skills
  - India
    - Mumbai
  - California
    - Redwood City
    - San Diego

What do you think?

Regards,
Mary

Email with Overbulleting

Do not do this in email, or in any kind of writing. It is too much. This starts to look like a technical schematic instead of an instance of human communication. Bullets can actually make simple ideas more complicated. Most people don't enjoy reading long word lists.

Here is a much-improved version of the email above—and it still has bullets!

To:	Joan Smith <joan.smith@xyz-inc.com>
From:	Mary Samuels <mary.samuels@xyz-inc.com>
Subject:	Training Needs for Staff

Good morning, Joan.

I've summarized below some training needs for our staff.

- executive presence training for new hires in Cleveland and Toledo
- writing training for senior managers in Cleveland
- grammar training for nonnative speakers in Tokyo, Dallas, and Houston
- grammar training for native speakers in multiple cities
- spreadsheet training in Mumbai, Redwood City, and San Diego

What do you think?

Thank you,
Mary

Revised Email with Readable Bulleting

4.2 Explain Your Attachments

If you attach something to an email, it is usually a good practice to include a line in the email telling the recipient what you've attached.

Before you send an attachment, double-check that you have attached the right file. Open it just to be sure.

Don't send emails like this:

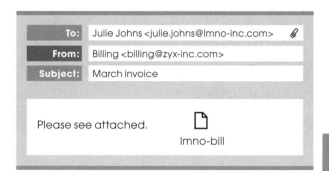

4

There is no searchable text, no friendly text—just an invoice. Besides being rude, this email is actually less likely to get paid, because it looks almost like spam and will not exactly proclaim its presence in an inbox full of thousands of email messages.

This revised version is much more effective.

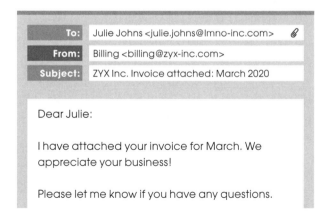

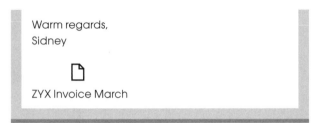

Warm regards,
Sidney

ZYX Invoice March

4.3 Emailing a Letter and Resume

People sometimes want to send a carefully formatted cover letter with a resume, but they want to email it. Then they end up with something like the following:

To: Manny Ramirez <manny.ramirez@zyx-hotel.com>

From: Louise Thomas <louise.thomas@lmno-inc.com>

Subject: Seeking management position

Dear Mr. Ramirez:

I have attached a cover letter and resume about my interest in a position at your hotel. Please see attachments for more information.

Thank you,
Louise Thomas

Too Many Attachments, Too Little Temptation

This is not a good approach; it is not at all enticing to someone who doesn't know you, or even someone who does. It is inconvenient, too: you have to open an email to get to the letter, which will probably be a little duplicative of the email, and then you get to the resume, which will be duplicative of the letter, which will be duplicative of the email.

Don't do it! Give up your dreams of perfect letter formatting! Turn the cover letter into an email and you will have just one attachment: your resume. Shown here is a far more seductive version of the original email.

To: Manny Ramirez <manny.ramirez@zyx-hotel.com>

From: Louise Thomas <louise.thomas@lmno-inc.com>

Subject: Seeking management position at Hotel ZYX

Dear Mr. Ramirez:

I am interested in a management position at your hotel. The recent news coverage fascinated me, and I am intrigued by the fact that you have attracted visitors from all over the world to this small Illinois town.

I worked in hotel management in Chicago for seven years, but I am also a polyglot who speaks seven languages fluently. I have been looking for a position for some time where I could combine those skills. I have an MBA from Cornell and live and work right down the street from your hotel in the downtown area.

I have attached my resume and would be glad to meet with you to discuss possible opportunities in more detail. Thank you for your time!

Sincerely,
Louise Thomas

One Attachment, Made Enticing

4.4 Informational Stinginess in Email

There are people who never seem to write more than a line or two, no matter how complicated an issue is. Extracting information from them is difficult and unpleasant, because they dole it out in microdoses.

Here is an example of a dialogue of this nature.

To:	Fritz Starck <fritz.starck@zyx-inc.com>
From:	Jean Arnold <jean.arnold@zyx-inc.com>
Subject:	Purchase Order Process

Hi Fritz,

I am having trouble with the purchase order process. The main screen is requiring me to enter a department number, and I don't have one. Could you tell me how I get that?

In addition, whenever I click Save on Field 11, I get an error message. I've attached a screenshot. What do you suggest?

Finally, is there any way to expedite the process? We need this item in four weeks, and I am concerned that we won't be able to get it in time.

Thank you,
Jean

The Start of a Frustrating Dialogue

To:	Jean Arnold <jean.arnold@zyx-inc.com>
From:	Fritz Starck <fritz.starck@zyx-inc.com>
Subject:	re: Purchase Order Process

I forwarded the screenshot to Rana. Sorry about that.

Frustrating Dialogue Is Underway

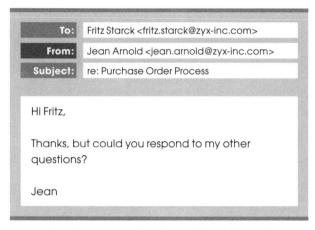

To: Fritz Starck <fritz.starck@zyx-inc.com>
From: Jean Arnold <jean.arnold@zyx-inc.com>
Subject: re: Purchase Order Process

Hi Fritz,

Thanks, but could you respond to my other questions?

Jean

Further Information Extraction Attempt

To: Jean Arnold <jean.arnold@zyx-inc.com>
From: Fritz Starck <fritz.starck@zyx-inc.com>
Subject: re: Purchase Order Process

We can't expedite.

Another Inadequate Reply

Four emails and Jean still doesn't have the answers she needs. One way to reduce the likelihood of this outcome is to number the questions, as shown here:

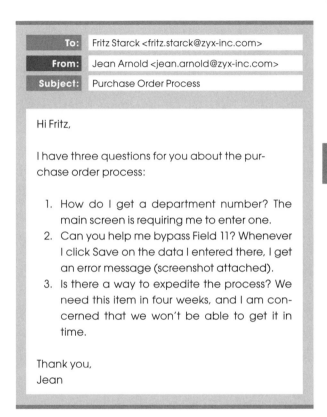

To: Fritz Starck <fritz.starck@zyx-inc.com>

From: Jean Arnold <jean.arnold@zyx-inc.com>

Subject: Purchase Order Process

Hi Fritz,

I have three questions for you about the purchase order process:

1. How do I get a department number? The main screen is requiring me to enter one.
2. Can you help me bypass Field 11? Whenever I click Save on the data I entered there, I get an error message (screenshot attached).
3. Is there a way to expedite the process? We need this item in four weeks, and I am concerned that we won't be able to get it in time.

Thank you,
Jean

4

A More Disasterproof Email

Bulletproof that email! The respondent can then simply place answers after your questions. If this still doesn't work, there is always the phone or a desk drive-by.

4.5 Bad News and Diplomacy

When you need to tell someone something negative at work, try to conquer the natural human discomfort at being the bearer of bad tidings. Be diplomatic but straightforward.

Following is an example of frustrating, business-damaging indirectness, with the bad and most important news hidden at the end.

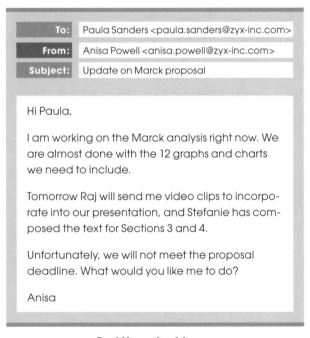

> **To:** Paula Sanders <paula.sanders@zyx-inc.com>
>
> **From:** Anisa Powell <anisa.powell@zyx-inc.com>
>
> **Subject:** Update on Marck proposal
>
> Hi Paula,
>
> I am working on the Marck analysis right now. We are almost done with the 12 graphs and charts we need to include.
>
> Tomorrow Raj will send me video clips to incorporate into our presentation, and Stefanie has composed the text for Sections 3 and 4.
>
> Unfortunately, we will not meet the proposal deadline. What would you like me to do?
>
> Anisa

Bad News Avoidance

Anisa doesn't get to the important part—that the entire deadline is about to be missed—until the end of the email. That needs to be the lead. Here is a revised version that provides similar information but neither dissembles nor defers. Trust, once again, is a foundation of effective writing.

4

To:	Paula Sanders <paula.sanders@zyx-inc.com>
From:	Anisa Powell <anisa.powell@zyx-inc.com>
Subject:	Problem with deadline for Marck proposal

Hi Paula,

Raj, Stefanie and I have been working on the Marck proposal since Saturday when we got the RFP, but we do not feel we can meet the deadline. How would you like to proceed?

This is where we are now:

- We are almost done with the 12 graphs and charts we need to include.
- Tomorrow Raj will get me the video clips to incorporate into our presentation.
- Stefanie has composed the text for Sections 3 and 4, but we are still missing about 10-15 pages of content that she hasn't had time to write.

I'm very sorry and would like to figure out how we can participate in this proposal process. I'd be glad to call the client.

My apologies,
Anisa

An Email That Confesses the Bad News Up Front

4.6 Sudden Attacks of Formality

If you regularly call someone by first name and have a friendly relationship with them in real life, you should not send them an email taking five steps backwards. This is an example of such an email.

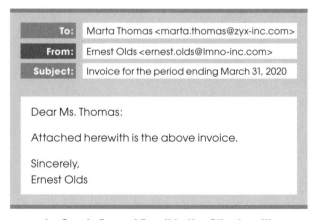

To:	Marta Thomas <marta.thomas@zyx-inc.com>
From:	Ernest Olds <ernest.olds@lmno-inc.com>
Subject:	Invoice for the period ending March 31, 2020

Dear Ms. Thomas:

Attached herewith is the above invoice.

Sincerely,
Ernest Olds

An Overly Formal Email to the Client—with an Invoice, Too!

In the example shown here, Ernest has addressed a client whom he has met in real life, and whom he addresses regularly by first name, as *Ms. Thomas*. He does it while *billing* her. Don't try to sound legalistic, especially when you are not actually a lawyer, and especially not while trying to extract money from someone you know.

Here is a much-improved version.

4

To:	Marta Thomas <marta.thomas@zyx-inc.com>
From:	Ernest Olds <ernest.olds@lmno-inc.com>
Subject:	Invoice for the period ending March 31, 2019

Dear Marta:

Attached is an invoice for the period ending March 31. As always, I very much appreciate your business, and I look forward to working with you again in the coming quarter.

Best regards,
Ernest

A Courteous, Friendly Email to the Client

4.7 Don't Put Disparate Topics in the Same Email

It is usually best to stick to one theme per email. In the next example, the writer fails to take this advice and combines a message about a report he has been working on with an apology for arriving late to a morning meeting.

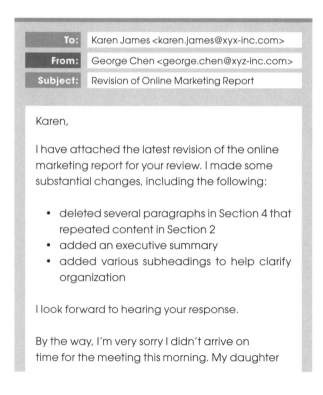

To: Karen James <karen.james@xyx-inc.com>

From: George Chen <george.chen@xyz-inc.com>

Subject: Revision of Online Marketing Report

Karen,

I have attached the latest revision of the online marketing report for your review. I made some substantial changes, including the following:

- deleted several paragraphs in Section 4 that repeated content in Section 2
- added an executive summary
- added various subheadings to help clarify organization

I look forward to hearing your response.

By the way, I'm very sorry I didn't arrive on time for the meeting this morning. My daughter

has bronchitis, and I had to take her to the
pediatrician on my way to work.

Regards,
George

Message That Can't Easily Be Forwarded

4

The first part of the email discusses a revision
of an online marketing report, a subject likely to be
of interest to other employees of the company. It is
quite possible, therefore, that the message will be forwarded. If the writer did a good job on the revision
mentioned in the email, the forwarding may well
benefit him professionally.

Unfortunately, though, if this email is forwarded in
its current form, the allusion to his tardiness will automatically be passed on as well. Instead of providing a
purely positive reflection of his efforts on behalf of the
company—exemplified by the report—the email will
inform people who would never have known it otherwise
that he was tardy to a meeting that morning. The email
also contains personal information about family that the
writer may not wish to share with others at his firm.

The writer would be better off doing one of two
things: (1) splitting the email into two messages, one
addressing the report and another apologizing for the

tardiness, or (2) sending an email about the report and apologizing in person or over the phone for the tardiness. In either case, the content relating to the report could then be forwarded to people who may be impressed by it. They will not hear about tardiness, bronchitis, or other personal matters.

In a second example, shown below, the recipient is the sender's client. This email is polite and clear, but it is less than ideal from a practical point of view. By covering two separate and unrelated issues—an upcoming project and an unpaid invoice—each of which requires the client to undertake a separate action, the writer reduces the chance that both actions will occur.

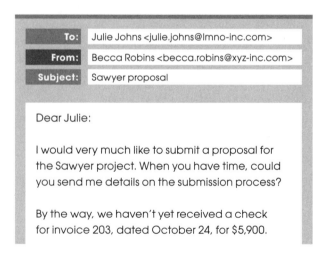

To:	Julie Johns <julie.johns@lmno-inc.com>
From:	Becca Robins <becca.robins@xyz-inc.com>
Subject:	Sawyer proposal

Dear Julie:

I would very much like to submit a proposal for the Sawyer project. When you have time, could you send me details on the submission process?

By the way, we haven't yet received a check for invoice 203, dated October 24, for $5,900.

> Could you please let me know the status of this payment?
>
> Thank you,
> Becca

Message That Bundles Two Unrelated Ideas

The recipient may well take care of one thing and then forget about the other. Because of the reference to the unpaid invoice, the recipient may forward the email to the accounting department without remembering to answer the sender's question about the upcoming project. If the writer doesn't follow up quickly, she may lose the business!

In addition, the person in accounting who processes the sender's invoices really doesn't need to know that she is bidding on a new project. All the person in accounting needs is information on the late payment.

It is a sound business writing practice to include no more information in an email than is relevant to your relationship with the original recipient and anyone else to whom your message is likely to be forwarded.

4.8 Don't Write Like a Telegram

Another often problematic habit in email is to leave out words as though one is being charged for them, like in an old-fashioned telegram. This section refers to words that are necessary grammatically, such as articles (*a*, *an*, and *the*) and direct objects.

For example, certain verbs require a direct object to complete their meaning, but direct objects are frequently omitted by emailers seeking to save keystrokes. Here is an example of a sentence with a direct object:

The attorney reviewed the paper.

You can't just write "The attorney reviewed." It is incomplete. The verb needs the direct object. Below are two examples common in informal email.

Missing Direct Object

Please review attached.

Missing Article

Please review attached report.

The problem is, many people don't shift out of this mode when they are writing important emails that require more care and attention. In email messages, get in the habit of writing complete sentences with no missing parts.

Complete Thought

Please review the attached report.

Included below is an example of an email that is simply too stingy with words. Words are missing from all three sentences, multiple words are abbreviated, and the writer, Will, is apparently too tired to sign his whole name.

4

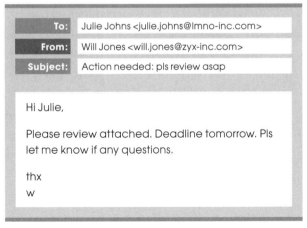

To:	Julie Johns <julie.johns@lmno-inc.com>
From:	Will Jones <will.jones@zyx-inc.com>
Subject:	Action needed: pls review asap

Hi Julie,

Please review attached. Deadline tomorrow. Pls let me know if any questions.

thx
w

Telegram-Like Email

Below is a courteous revision that required mere additional seconds to compose.

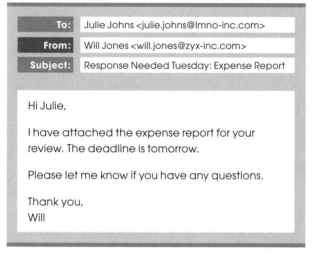

To: Julie Johns <julie.johns@lmno-inc.com>

From: Will Jones <will.jones@zyx-inc.com>

Subject: Response Needed Tuesday: Expense Report

Hi Julie,

I have attached the expense report for your review. The deadline is tomorrow.

Please let me know if you have any questions.

Thank you,
Will

Telegram Style Replaced with Human Style

Chapter 5

Mind Your Email Details

Minding the details of email—capitalization, punctuation, and so on—shows respect for the reader's time and ease. If you type unpunctuated, undercapitalized messages, you give the impression that the recipient's convenience is less important than your time—the very tiny amount of time it would take to fix these minor problems. Don't send that message!

Some of this discussion applies to other documents as well, but the focus is on idiosyncrasies seen most often in email.

5.1 Capitalization in Email Messages

Don't skip capital letters because it's easier for you. Avoiding the Shift key might save you some milliseconds every now and then, but incorrectly lowercase letters are confusing and unprofessional. Entirely lowercase subject lines look sloppy. Writing someone's name in all lowercase letters is rude.

The few people left in the world who still type messages in all caps are probably impervious to the following advice, but here goes anyway: NEVER TYPE IN ALL CAPS.

See how annoying that is?

All caps is kind of like saying to the reader, "I can't possibly be bothered to click the Shift key when I need a capital letter, so to save myself the trouble, you get this entire screaming message."

At this point in internet and email history, all-caps typing looks very unsophisticated and is also associated with internet trolls.

5.2 Email Font Should Be Boring

For the contents of your business email, avoid unusual or eccentric fonts. Keep it simple. Use black. Keep the background white.

Justifiable exceptions to these font guidelines can be found in a professionally designed signature file, created under the guidance of a corporate art department or designer.

It is fine, though, to use the same font for your signature file that you use throughout the text of your email. You can also set off the signature by making it a little smaller than the rest of your email, or adding a simple design element like a line above it, or perhaps using a dark gray font in it rather than black.

5.3 Exclamation Points in Email

Exclamation points tend to be far more numerous in email (and messaging) than in other business documents. That makes sense, because in email, people are often trying to recreate the rhythms of spoken language. People email in a conversational mode; exclamation points are a way to show enthusiasm for their subject.

Unfortunately, an email message full of exclamation points tends to read as unprofessional.

Hi Blake!

I love your report! It's great! I wish I could write like you!

Sandy

The recipient of this message will probably be happy anyway, because the email is full of compliments. Nonetheless, use exclamation points sparingly. Punctuating with 100% exclamation points is just a little bit too much enthusiasm.

5.4 Ellipses and Dashes ... Running Amok

Ellipses (...) and dashes have been steadily expanding their domain over the past couple of decades. Be careful about using these in informal ways in what should be more formal communications.

The main formal use of the ellipsis is to indicate missing words in quoted material. That's it! In email, however, ellipses are often used casually for suspense, for a break in thought, and to mean "et cetera." Avoid those uses.

The dash is a more flexible piece of punctuation, but distribute your dashes with care. Don't use dashes just because you are not sure what punctuation should actually go there. Dashes are used mostly for (1) clarity amid a competing comma cluster and (2) drama. They are not meant to be all-purpose punctuation substitutes for when you don't know what really belongs at a particular pause.

Here are examples of overly informal ellipsis and dash use in email.

I wonder if she'll call...

Bill definitely won't attend...it wouldn't be productive—too much to do.

Let's order tomatoes, pickles, mustard...

Now, here are improved revisions of the samples above:

I wonder if she'll call.

Bill definitely won't attend; it wouldn't be productive. He has too much to do.

Let's order tomatoes, pickles, mustard, etc.

5.5 Aggressive Punctuation!!!

Punctuation is sometimes used as a kind of weapon. Perhaps you yourself have been the victim of a punctuation assault, as in the following examples:

Where is the document I requested??

I asked you to get here by 4:00!!!

When are you going to deliver the folders?!

In general, avoid aggressive punctuation, which we will define as the combination of multiple consecutive exclamation points and/or question marks (instead of the usual allotment of one) to demonstrate anger, irritation, or urgency. In business communications, such punctuation will often be received as inflammatory or rude.

If you need a document right away, use authoritative, professional language to request it. Do not rely on punctuation to do your dirty work.

5.6 Abbreviations and Emojis

Use abbreviations, emoticons, and emojis with care, for two main reasons: (1) Some people won't understand them, and (2) They come across as unprofessional. Treat work email differently than you treat personal texting and chat.

> lol
>
> Thx.
>
> ☺
>
> :-)
>
> When r u going to arrive? c u there.
>
> I will be OOO until March 23.

OOO is "out of office," but to the uninitiated it might look like someone is having just a little bit too much fun. This kind of text-like talk is best confined to personal communications.

5.7 Responding to Careless Emailers

What should you do if someone—your supervisor, for instance—habitually sends you messages full of nonstandard capitalization and punctuation? Is it rude not to respond in kind? Could that perhaps seem like a criticism of the other person's email style?

No. When you are communicating in writing with someone you work for, it is important that you make the experience of reading your message as easy as possible. That doesn't mean you have to adopt an artificially formal style. A simple message such as this one is fine.

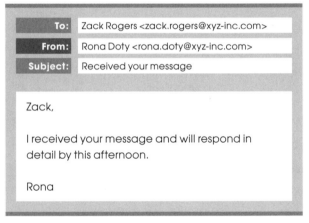

To: Zack Rogers <zack.rogers@xyz-inc.com>
From: Rona Doty <rona.doty@xyz-inc.com>
Subject: Received your message

Zack,

I received your message and will respond in detail by this afternoon.

Rona

A Brief but Courteous Email Message

Chapter 6

Special Topics in Email

E mail offers powerful communication capabilities—but also some attendant risks and challenges. This chapter addresses communication issues unique to email.

6.1 Copying Etiquette

Copy only people who need to be copied. Don't fall into the trap of using email to create a long and many-layered electronic paper trail.

True, if your friend Joe copies everyone on everything, no one will be able to complain that Joe didn't inform them of a particular event or detail. They will almost surely, however, complain that he is constantly wasting their time and irritating them with unnecessary emails.

Naturally you should copy managers who have requested that you copy them on certain types of communications. In addition, if your company or industry has procedures that must be followed (i.e., copying someone with a particular role relative to you), you should comply with those requirements.

Otherwise, you should generally copy only those people who truly need the information you are sending in a given email. Don't automatically emulate what your co-workers happen to be doing. For example, don't copy five of your colleagues just because you noticed that another of your co-workers—who has been at the firm a year longer than you have—did that on his last communication. Perhaps that person's judgment was flawed. The important question is whether those five colleagues really need the information you are sending.

Now it is time for some email math. If you put one person in the To field and seven people in the Cc field—just because you want to make sure anyone who would ever want to know the information you are sending gets it, even if you think it is unlikely they will care—and then you press Send, you will have just sent eight emails. Not one, but eight! Think about how much reading that means. Eight people will now have your email and will now have to tend to it. There is way too much frivolous copying in the world, so we should all do our part to minimize it.

If you copy people for legitimate reasons, that's fine. Just make sure, if the recipient in the To field doesn't know the copied person or people, that you explain who the copied people are and why you are copying them. Below is a sample email from Sue Jones to Jane Smith, and copying Tom Roberts, which does exactly that.

Email Copying a Manager

6.2 Minimize Use of "Reply All"

Imagine that you are one of 10 recipients on an email message. If you respond by clicking Reply All, the sender and the other nine original recipients will all receive your message.

If everyone needs to see your response, then Reply All is fine. If only the original sender needs to see it, though, don't impose your response unnecessarily on nine extra people.

If Reply suffices, it is almost always preferable to use that rather than Reply All. But there is a third choice, too.

Suppose a subset of the original group needs your response—perhaps the original sender plus three of the original recipients. In that case, you could click Reply All but then delete the other people's addresses from the To field before sending. Your response will then go just to an appropriate subset of the original group. A moment of careful thought on your end can save time for six people. Multiply that kind of thinking by many emails over the course of the year, and it's a huge difference.

6.3 The Ethics of Forwarding

A healthy sense of self-preservation should keep you from writing emails you wouldn't want to have forwarded to someone else. Email does get forwarded, so it is simply good defensive emailing to avoid saying anything inappropriate, contentious, or undiplomatic in a work-related message. This section, however, focuses on the act of forwarding itself—because forwarders too have responsibilities.

Don't forward an email message to someone without thinking first about whether the message will be useful to that person. Even if you think an emailed joke is hysterically funny, avoid forwarding it, or similar types of messages, to others at work. Your colleagues are unlikely to tell you if they find such messages annoying, and it is contrary to the spirit, and probably the letter, of many companies' policies on email use at work.

Whether it is acceptable to forward a work message depends on myriad factors, including the relationship between the writer and recipient, their relative status, and the content and context of the message. But in all cases it is important to remember that forwarding something private or sensitive is often likely to reflect poorly not only on the writer, but also on the person who forwards the message.

Proceed with caution when you forward an email from anyone, but be extra cautious when the email is from someone senior to you. In general, don't forward messages containing:

- **Personal content.** Professionals should not embed personal information in business emails, but when they do, think twice (or thrice) before passing it on.
- **Confidential information.** Be very careful in your treatment of sensitive personnel data or other business information.

- **Lengthy dialogues.** Don't forward a dialogue several pages long with a quick note at the top saying, "What do you think?" Instead, consider writing a synthesis of the key issues. If you do forward an email that contains a series of email exchanges, make sure the entire dialogue is appropriate for forwarding. There may be sensitive content farther down the page; check before sharing it with others.

- **Carelessly edited content.** Sometimes when colleagues are in a rush, they may write things that are not perfectly worded. Think about the original writer's intended audience before you blithely forward an email. It's just good relationship management. (You yourself, however, should still write everything as though it could be forwarded.)

6.4 Automatic Replies: Handle with Care

An automatic reply is the message people set up to go out automatically in response to any emails that arrive, often though not necessarily while they are out of the office.

If you make a mistake in one regular email in the course of a day, it is usually not going to be a catastrophe. If you make a mistake in an auto-reply, also sometimes called an auto-responder, that mistake may go out hundreds of times while you are lying on a beach in the Caribbean. Unfortunately, many people compose auto-replies in a rush right before they go away on a business trip or vacation. It is very difficult to write a good email while rushing.

Poor proofreading of an auto-reply caused a major US financial firm to send out a whole bunch of emails assuring job applicants that their submission had been *recieved* rather than *received*.

Below are some guidelines to keep in mind when you set up an auto-reply:

- Compose it ahead of time so that you are not too rushed to review it carefully.
- Make sure the auto-reply is turned off as soon as you return from your trip, or wherever you happen to have been. It is undesirable, on January 24, to still have messages going out announcing that you will return from your vacation on January 2.
- Don't use abbreviations such as OOO for "out of office." You have to type it only once, so write actual words that everyone is sure to understand.

Here is an example of a professional auto-reply.

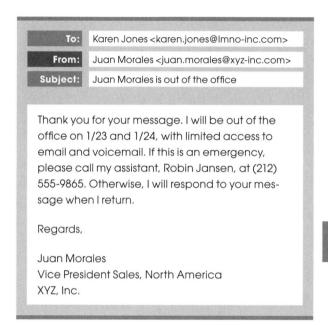

To: Karen Jones <karen.jones@lmno-inc.com>

From: Juan Morales <juan.morales@xyz-inc.com>

Subject: Juan Morales is out of the office

Thank you for your message. I will be out of the office on 1/23 and 1/24, with limited access to email and voicemail. If this is an emergency, please call my assistant, Robin Jansen, at (212) 555-9865. Otherwise, I will respond to your message when I return.

Regards,

Juan Morales
Vice President Sales, North America
XYZ, Inc.

Professional Auto-Reply

For auto-replies, consider limiting the information you include in your signature, as in this sample, since those messages will be going out not only to colleagues but also to strangers and spammers who might email you in your absence.

6.5 Blind Copying: Benefits and Risks

Blind copying enables you to copy someone on a message without allowing the main recipient to see that anyone else is receiving it. It is the Bcc field (standing for *blind carbon copy*) on an email.

Use blind copying for the following:

- mass emails where you don't want everyone to know who is on your mailing list
- mass emails where there is a risk that a thoughtless person will hit Reply All, thereby informing every other person on that list that the person wants to order a pastrami sandwich for the upcoming luncheon meeting "except please hold the mayonnaise, b/c I hate mayonnaise"

The Bcc field can be very useful for certain types of group mailings. When you send out messages to multiple people who do not know one another—for instance, a dozen of your company's vendors—you can use the Bcc field to ensure that their email addresses are not revealed. It is good business to respect the privacy of people you email.

Otherwise, be conservative about using the blind-copying feature, as it is sometimes employed in ways that test the limits of business etiquette and ethics. Generally you should not blind copy someone if the recipient in the To field would be disturbed to discover that that person was surreptitiously included in the communication. If the blind copying does not serve a legitimate and ethical business purpose, avoid it.

6.6 Don't Email in Anger

Don't email inflammatory content. That includes angry comments, rude comments, passive-aggressive comments, and a million other things that people inexplicably email at work that they should never be emailing at work.

If you sense that an email dialogue is becoming confrontational, stop communicating about the topic online and have a phone conversation or face-to-face discussion with the person. It is much harder to communicate effectively about sensitive topics through the medium of the computer than it is in person or over the phone. By talking things through, you are more likely to keep a situation from spiraling out of control.

It often takes a ridiculously long time to compose good emails when you are mad, so talking it out may well be a time-saver, too.

6.7 Handheld Devices Are No Excuse

Workers on the move enjoy the convenience of phones and other devices that enable them to send and receive email wherever they are. Unfortunately, it is not easy to compose articulate messages on small devices. Thumbs are big and phones are not.

Your mobile lifestyle, however, is not an excuse for a lack of clarity or an unprofessional format. You should in most cases still adhere to the standard guidelines for appropriate email messages, setting up proper signature files, proofing for grammar and punctuation, and so on.

For email that doesn't require an urgent reply, consider waiting until you are sitting at your computer. If your work permits—and maybe it doesn't—you might consider using the device primarily for reading messages and not so much for writing.

6.8 Urgent Email: How Urgent Is It?

You have the ability to show that a message is of high importance by marking it with a red exclamation point or some other urgent-looking indicator, with the precise choice of indicator depending on the email client you use to send and receive email. That doesn't mean you should actually do it, though.

This feature tends to be abused by senders whose idea of a high priority departs from their readers' idea of a high priority. Often a very significant percentage of a department's emergency emails come from a single person, without there being any reason for that person to have more emergencies than the next.

Unless you are absolutely certain that the situation is urgent, don't mark an email as high-priority—particularly if it is going to someone you work for.

Even when something is urgent, you have alternatives to marking it urgent. For example, you can send a regular email and then follow up with a call. Don't ever fall into the habit of using urgent markers to compensate for a failure to track your own tasks and deadlines. Often overuse of the urgent email feature publicly signals a time management problem.

6

6.9 The Etiquette of Read Receipts

A read receipt, which notifies the sender of an email when the message has been opened, is another frequently abused technological tool. Use these receipts only if absolutely necessary. They are surely necessary only a very small percentage of the time they are used across the US.

Many readers find them intrusive, though they will be much more receptive to a read receipt if a message is critical for business or legal reasons. Otherwise, people don't necessarily like having someone know when they have seen an email; they may consider the management of their email correspondence to be a private matter.

Finally, a read receipt doesn't prove that someone has *read* your email; it merely demonstrates that they have opened it. The mere opening of your email is not going to advance your purpose. If you need someone to take action on what you sent, you are no further along than you would have been without the receipt.

6.10 Reducing Email Volume

Many people freely admit to taking a CYA approach to email. In case you are unfamiliar with this abbreviation, it stands for "cover your ass."

Excessive CYA emailing is a blight on the workplace. Don't overemail to make yourself feel safe. Don't be the anxious person who overdocuments everything "just in case." Don't become the person whose emails people dread because they are so often a waste of time to read.

CYA emailing is a habit for the fearful. Be brave. Send what you need to send. Do not send more.

6.11 Reader Responsibilities

Amid a flood of incoming email, people who use it for work must be vigilant about their handling of individual messages. Here are some guidelines for you.

1. Be cool.

Don't overreact to incoming email, because that puts you at risk of letting others set your tone. Stay in charge of your own tone. When people write to you rudely, or in a way that you perceive as rude, try to stay calm and keep in mind that, even though writers should be polite, not everyone has the writing skills to do that, and most of the time, people mean no harm. Don't overinterpret small details, either. The fact that someone did not put a *Hi* before your name is likely meaningless; some people don't put the word *Hi* before people's names.

2. Don't file and delete recklessly.

If you arrive at the office in the morning and encounter 100 new email messages, it is natural to want to take care of them efficiently. However, if you go through them too quickly, there is a chance you will make mistakes. Go slowly enough that you can avoid misfilings and accidental deletions of important messages.

3. Skimming isn't reading.

You can't eyeball a computer screen and take in all the content someone has sent you, or all the mistakes you may be about to send someone. Read with care.

4. Reading half an email isn't equivalent to reading the whole email.

Address all of the sender's questions or concerns. If there are two questions and you answer one, you get way less than 50% of the credit for answering, because of the irritation you will have just produced. The original emailer will have to send a follow-up email to extract the answer to the second question. If four messages are necessary instead of two, your half-reading habit will not have saved anyone time—not even you.

5. Respond quickly when it's important.

If you receive an urgent email that requires a prompt response—say, within a day—consider sending a quick email to say you have received the email and are working on a response. Be a stress-reducer, not a stress-producer.

You might also want to indicate when you expect to send the response. Mark a reminder on your calendar or set an alert so that you remember to follow through.

If for some reason you can't or don't respond to an important message quickly enough (and how quickly is quickly enough will depend on the context), apologize for the delay.

Chapter 7

The Creative Process:
Idea Generation

Most email is very short. Longer email messages and other document types usually require more thought than a simple email reading "Hi Giuliana, please meet me at 4 p.m. in the employee lounge. Thanks!"

Good writing is impossible without good ideas. If you start composing too quickly, without thinking first, you may find you are cutting off some of your creative energy before it has a chance to express itself.

To help ensure a productive experience, think of writing more complex documents as a three-part process: prewriting, writing, and rewriting. Most people focus too much on the writing stage at the expense of the prewriting and rewriting stages.

Prewriting is important because it helps ensure that you consider a full spectrum of ideas before you start your first draft. It can consist of various activities, including the ones described below.

7.1 Brainstorming

Take out a piece of paper (or open a new file on your computer) and list any and all thoughts you have on your topic. Phrases and sentence fragments are fine, even preferable; at this stage the last thing you should concern yourself with is grammar.

Also, do not worry about whether your ideas are good or bad. Turn off that critical voice in your head, and simply write down everything that occurs to you, from details to general ideas to possible counterarguments.

If you are self-critical before you even get something down on paper, you may get in the way of the free association that could lead you to even better ideas.

7.2 Freewriting

Freewriting exercises can be helpful for people who suffer from severe writer's block. As with brainstorming, take out a blank piece of paper—or, if you are electronically inclined, open a new file—and just start writing about your topic.

The only rule of freewriting is: do not stop writing! Make yourself write for at least 10 minutes without stopping. Set a timer to keep yourself honest.

Unlike brainstorming, freewriting involves writing in more or less standard sentences and, if you like, paragraphs. If you run out of ideas, simply write something like this:

> I don't know what to say I need some coffee my foot hurts etc. I wish I knew punctuation rules

> better. I am v anxious about this deadline plus I
> don't know the subject, what do I know about
> automotive supplies

And so on, until something occurs to you. Once again, do not worry about grammar, spelling, the quality of your ideas, or even relevance. Just write.

In prewriting, you unlock your creativity. Maybe some of the things you write down won't be relevant. Maybe the majority won't be relevant! That's fine. At least you will have some words to work with—a crucial first step! *Some* words on a page are more reassuring than no words on a page.

7.3 Research and Notetaking

Good writing depends on a solid grasp of the material; without it, a writer can't communicate clearly with other people. In a professional environment, though, people must often write about topics that aren't initially familiar to them, so if you find yourself in this situation, don't despair!

You have company everywhere.

Begin by making every effort to educate yourself about your subject. Time spent acquiring information is time well spent. You do not need to be writing in order to advance your writing goals. Don't rush.

If your writing project requires research, read about your topic online, in other documents your organization has published previously, in the news, or anywhere else it is appropriate and relevant for you to find reliable information.

You may want to interview colleagues, customers, or other people with experience and knowledge to help you gather necessary information. You will probably want to take notes throughout the research process.

Sometimes careful writers doing research end up with many multiples of the amount of information they ultimately use in the finished document. There's nothing wrong with that. You need *authority* before you can *author* something. Collecting information helps give you that authority.

Knowing a lot also helps you write faster and more confidently. Value the nonwriting part of the writing process.

7.4 Outlining

Once you have completed any necessary research, brainstormed, and/or tried freewriting exercises, examine what you have so far and start to consider what you might include in your document and how it could be arranged.

Some people like to create an outline, which can be an extremely valuable thing to do before writing a draft. You can put the main idea at the top of the page and then number subpoints below it, adding subpoints of the subpoints as needed.

Outlining requires a sense of structure that not everyone will have at this prewriting stage, however. Suppose you're not ready to outline. In that case, you can instead read through the research you've collected, or perhaps look at a list of ideas you created through brainstorming.

If you take that list and start crossing off irrelevant ideas, marking ideas that you would like to use, drawing arrows to connect related points, and so on, you may begin to get a sense of possible structure for your memo, report, or whatever document you happen to be writing.

Some people just can't outline in advance. They are too distracted by the details to see the big picture. No problem! If you don't outline ahead, you may end up with a messier, less organized draft, but that's fine—as long as you spend the time you need to edit the draft into good organizational shape before you impose it on your readers.

7.5 Try Going Tech-Free

Some people may benefit from a technology-free prewriting experience—just them and a pad of paper. Many people are so accustomed to computers now that they cannot bear to write on paper, but if you have chronic writer's block, try an experiment: do at least some of your brainstorming, freewriting, research, outlining, etc., away from a computer, with no technology nearby.

Sometimes the brain–pencil or brain–pen connection outperforms the brain–keyboard connection. It is common for professional writers to do at least some idea generation away from a computer.

At the very least, writing in peace on paper will take you away from the temptations of multitasking: checking messages, checking social media, checking the news, etc. Without good and careful thinking, there can be no good writing.

7

Chapter 8

The Structure of Longer Documents

8

A large percentage of what people write at work today is a few lines long, sent through email or messaging services. It is important to get to the point quickly in those communications, but they don't necessarily adhere to the kind of document structure teachers tended to focus on in English classes: a longer composition of multiple paragraphs.

That's what this chapter is for! Longer documents—whether they are memos, or reports, or longish emails—should generally have an introduction, a body consisting of multiple body paragraphs, and a conclusion.

8.1 The Thesis and the Introduction

The introduction should help the reader understand what will be covered in the body of a document, meaning everything between the introduction and the conclusion. It should contain your thesis, or main idea. If you can't express that main idea in a sentence or two, you should keep thinking, writing, and rewriting until you can. This holds true whether you are composing a business letter, a proposal, or any other type of document, including email.

Many people are diligent about trying to convey their main point but then neglect a critical second purpose of an introduction: to engage the reader. Upon finishing your introduction, your reader should want to continue reading. Try to avoid dull, self-referential language like this:

> The purpose of this report is to tell you about X.
> In this memo I would like to tell you about Y.

Instead, just start talking about X or Y.

An introduction does not have a minimum or maximum length, though most good introductions of brief to midsized documents consist of two to four sentences.

In some cases—for example, in complex reports—the introduction may extend to a few paragraphs, but the vast majority of openings should be confined to a single paragraph.

Some people write their introductions last, after they have completed a draft of a document. Other people find it more productive to write a working introduction first. Later they revise it, perhaps repeatedly, to make sure it describes the point of the document in a concise, clear, and interesting way.

Let's try an example. Imagine that you are a senior executive at a company called the Peaceful Home

Corporation, and that you are coming to the end of the first quarter. At your company, you are responsible for writing a quarterly memo, several pages long, that goes out to all department heads throughout the firm and gives an overview of how the past quarter went. Below are the points the memo would cover:

- First-quarter sales were 12% lower than for the first quarter of last year.
- In January, Peaceful Home lost several senior executives to a competitor.
- Over the past nine months, the company has diversified its offerings, expanding into three new areas: bathroom fixtures, small kitchen appliances, and garden tools.
- In those three new areas, sales for the quarter were significant, accounting for $43 million of the company's total quarterly sales of $420 million.
- Management expects sales to grow further in these three areas during the rest of the year.
- However, management expects demand to remain weak in most of its business lines over the next few quarters.

Below, based on this content, are samples of several introductions with common weaknesses. The sentence that seems to be the thesis is underlined in each.

Intro #1. Too General

> <u>This report describes how our first quarter went</u>.
> It will present quantitative information as well as
> personnel information.

This introduction does not characterize the quarter; it just tells you that the topic is the first quarter. The quarter could have been awful, or it could have been great; you can't tell. The paragraph is also dull. The writer seems tentative about making a statement. The first sentence appears to be the thesis, but it is inadequate; it gives you no insight into how things went.

8

Intro #2. Too Narrow

> <u>Sales were down 12% this quarter compared to
> last year</u>. Sales of new products were significant,
> though, accounting for $43 million of the
> company's total quarterly sales of $420 million.

This introduction is too narrow. The first sentence gives the impression that this memo will be a sales summary, but that's not the case. The thesis is so narrow that the reader will be surprised in the body of the document to come across information on the departed senior employees. The introduction is too glued to sales numbers.

Intro #3. Too Detailed and Too Long

<u>First-quarter sales were 12% lower than during the first quarter of last year</u>. In addition, in January, Peaceful Home lost several senior executives to a competitor. Over the past nine months, the company has diversified its offerings, expanding into three new areas: bathroom fixtures, small kitchen appliances, and garden tools. In those three new areas, sales for the quarter were significant, accounting for $43 million of the company's total quarterly sales of $420 million. Management expects sales to grow further in these three areas during the rest of the year, although sales are likely to remain weak in most of its business lines during the next several quarters.

The first sentence appears to be the thesis and is still too narrow, but the introduction is endless. It does not give an overview or shape to the material. It merely combines a bunch of information and tosses it at the reader. Mentioning all the details does not let you off the hook. Stand back from your details and take a stand on them! Shape them for the reader!

Intro #4. Too Positive

This quarter our newly diversified business lines have done really well, accounting for more than 10% of our overall sales. We expect those new areas to do well in the coming months. In addition, we have exciting new changes in our senior leadership. Although sales are down, we think we will do well in the coming quarters because of our new product areas.

8

No thesis is underlined here, because none is identifiable. The paragraph hops from one detail to the next. It is almost all positive spin: our new products did well, and the departure of senior executives has been turned into good news. The paragraph is dishonest. At best, the response among readers will be eye rolls. This is not a writer people can trust. We still have one try left, though!

Intro #5. A Much Improved Introduction

<u>The first quarter was a challenging but promising one for the Peaceful Home Corporation</u>. Despite an overall decline in sales and some management turnover, we saw significant growth in several new business lines. Even amid what will likely be ongoing weak demand, we expect these new areas to continue to flourish, providing a powerful competitive advantage in the months and years ahead.

The first sentence is a solid thesis. It doesn't merely tell you that the memo will tell you about the quarter, as the first sample introduction did; it actually indicates that there were both ups and downs. In addition, unlike the second and third samples, the thesis is broad enough, without being so broad as to be useless, that it sets up the writer to elaborate on numbers, people, products, and prospects in the body. Finally, and critically, the paragraph is honest.

8.2 Don't Use Transitional Expressions as Organizational Bandages

Today many working professionals have a writing process that goes something like this: Open a new file, start typing, keep typing until several pages have been completed, go to lunch with the intention of revising afterwards, return to one's desk, read over the document, decide it's not so bad after all, add a hard return in the middle of an extra-long paragraph, add a few transitional expressions to make the ideas flow better (an *in addition* here, a *however* there, a *moreover* somewhere else), run the grammar-checker and spell-checker, attach the document to an email, and press Send.

Transitional expressions are useful, but they cannot cure bad structure. Adding a *furthermore* to the beginning of a sentence to try to make it sound as though it is related to the previous sentence, even when it really isn't, is futile. In fact, it is worse than futile: it is confusing and annoying for the reader. For example:

> Last year, the company outsourced its fulfillment services to a company in Tennessee. Furthermore, it will be expanding its warehouse in Indiana.

Those two sentences are not connected logically, and a *furthermore* cannot resolve that. Using words that don't fit will confuse the reader.

To fix organizational weaknesses, look carefully at content, and consider whether the way the ideas are ordered actually makes sense.

8.3 Order of Ideas

The order of ideas in a piece of business writing varies based on content and goals, and may vary from section to section. However, your ideas should unfold in a way that is as easy as possible for the reader to understand.

Human beings like to tell stories in order. We do it all the time, from the time we start speaking: *First this happened, then that happened, then this other thing happened, and so on.* In stories, we the listeners usually learn things in the order in which they occurred.

Unfortunately, that is often *not* the best order for business content. A long email that tells you everything that went wrong with a piece of technology start to finish, and then tells you at the bottom of the page what has been done about it, and what you need to do, is an example of telling a story in chronological order. That's not how most busy people want to be informed of developments at work.

Instead, the best approach for the body is often to put the most important ideas first. Let's say this is your thesis in an introduction to a memo: "We need to renovate our employee lunchroom."

There are three main reasons you want this renovation:

1. The paint color is very 1970s, and you feel it needs an update.
2. You have increased staff by 8% since the last renovation, and there often isn't room for everyone to sit down.
3. There is a hole in the floor, and you are at risk of lawsuits if you don't fix it.

You are absolutely not going to begin with #1. That is the least important. The walls may be a really disgusting beige, but #2 and #3 are the big ideas. Decide which of those is bigger, begin with that, then move to the next biggest idea, and end with the paint color. Aesthetics are not irrelevant—one's work environment is important—but the other two problems are weightier.

Sometimes this most-important-idea-first structure won't work. You may need to explain a chain of logically interconnected ideas.

Point A → Point B → Point C → Point D

With this structure, each point follows logically from the previous idea and leads logically to the next. Point A might not be the biggest idea, but you may need it to explain Point B, and so on. It's cumulative.

You might see this structure in a technical document for a business audience, where you are explaining complex ideas to people who are unfamiliar with your subject matter. To succeed, you must think like a teacher, introducing ideas one at a time to your audience and explaining each one clearly before you move on to the next. You may actually end up developing your most important idea in later body paragraphs—after you have explained all the preceding concepts the reader must grasp in order to understand your big idea.

Training materials and user guides are examples of document types that frequently rely on this organizational scheme. One challenge in such material is momentum: you have to keep people engaged as you proceed step by step. Good writing—concise, dynamic, simple—helps. More on that later in this book!

8.4 Detail and the Body Paragraph

A body paragraph—in other words, any paragraph falling between the introduction and conclusion—should typically contain one main idea, called the topic sentence, on which the writer elaborates. There are exceptions, but many paragraphs follow this format—and many of those that don't, should.

You must explain your ideas adequately in the body of your document; in other words, you must develop them. The reader should not have to labor to understand what you mean; rather, you—the writer—should labor so the reader doesn't have to.

Thus, complex points must be allotted time and space sufficient for the reader to understand them. General statements should be supported with details and examples.

Detail-oriented people often really, truly love their details. They get attached to them. Abstract thinkers may be more comfortable with the big picture. In a good body paragraph, both inclinations need to be involved.

Consider the following paragraph from a hypothetical email:

> We must do a better job of meeting customer
> needs. For example, we have to respond more

> quickly and professionally to customer requests
> for assistance.

What does "more quickly and professionally" mean? It will certainly mean different things to different people.

Below is a new and improved version:

> We must do a better job of meeting customer
> needs. When a customer calls or emails with
> a problem or complaint, we need to resolve
> the issue within 24 hours. In addition, we should
> follow up with a phone call within five days of
> an initial inquiry to ensure that the customer is
> satisfied with the resolution.

The revised version contains concrete, useful details. Although the first version did not develop its main idea, the second does. The second is more likely to lead to action.

Another situation where details matter is annual reviews of employees. Let's say you are trying to help your employee, Dennis, improve his writing.

Saying "Dennis needs to improve his writing" is not going to do the job. Try to pick specific goals that will help your employee make specific improvements.

Perhaps you could add something like "Dennis's report introductions are usually a page instead of a couple of paragraphs. I would like Dennis to limit himself to 125 words in his introductions, and to make sure he has a thesis—an idea summarizing the overall point—within the first two or three sentences." Now you and Dennis have something to work with.

8.5 The Length of the Body Paragraph

Imagine you have to read a report on your business unit's performance during the third quarter. Nearly every paragraph takes up about half of a single-spaced page—page after page after page. What is the effect on you, the reader?

Maybe dread, because readers like white space as well as visual and thematic breaks. Have you ever received an email message that consists of a single page-long paragraph?

Pretty much no one is happy to discover such an email in their inbox. The big block of text means the writer has most likely included too many ideas in each paragraph, thus leaving it up to the recipient to sort out which sentences go together and what the relationship among the various ideas is.

8

When you signal the start of a new paragraph (by indenting, or skipping a line, or both), you are signaling to the reader the start of a new thought. Paragraphing is an example of how form—in other words, the appearance of a document—supports content.

Now, imagine you are reading a report that strings together a series of extremely short paragraphs. That can be a problem, too. Writers who overuse short paragraphs often create a choppy, disjointed effect.

As in most things, moderation is often the best approach. You can have long paragraphs, you can have short paragraphs, but don't have too many of one or the other. Your paragraphs should be complete and they should be manageable.

8.6 Conclusions for Longer Documents

Unless they follow a strict template with defined sections and headings, business documents usually need a conclusion that reminds the reader of the writer's key points. For most, a good conclusion will be a paragraph in length, though just as with the introduction, a longer, more complex document may require a somewhat longer conclusion.

In creating a conclusion, one of the biggest challenges writers face is how to close a document without simply repeating, in the same or similar words, what has already appeared in the introduction or elsewhere in the document.

Remember, though, when your readers reach the conclusion, they will have traveled some distance since the introduction. You, the writer, will presumably have explained your ideas, provided examples and details, and left your readers more educated about your topic than they were at the beginning. Because of your readers' greater understanding, you can go a step further in your conclusion than you did in your introduction.

For example, in the conclusion of a report you might tie together your main ideas while commenting on their implication for the future. In a memo, you might summarize issues discussed in the body of the document while also emphasizing for the readers what action you would like them to take.

If you are stuck, take a step back and think about the larger practical and philosophical importance of what you have written. Why does it matter? What do you want your reader to do or think about your topic? Your conclusion is an opportunity to bring home the piece's significance in a way that is difficult to do at the beginning, when you are introducing brand new ideas.

Chapter 9

Notes on Different Document Types

9

T his chapter provides specific guidance and cautionary notes for documents other than email: business letters, presentation slides, thank-you notes, proposals, and more.

9.1 Business Letters Aren't Dead

A letter on nice letterhead has an impact difficult to replicate in email. This sample includes tips on effective letter writing.

ZYX, Inc.
345 Arthropod Street
New York, NY 10024

September 28, 2020

Ms. Rona Jovino
The Grammar Group
127 Semicolon Street
New York, NY 10023

Dear Ms. Jovino:

I saw your recent article about email etiquette in the *Busby Post*. I was disappointed that you didn't mention business letters as well, because

I am concerned that the art of letter writing is a dying one. I would like to share some of my letter-related observations with you.

Many business letters I receive today lack a clear purpose in their first paragraph. Just like the thesis in a school essay, a letter should have a sentence in its opening paragraph that makes clear what the purpose of the letter is. If the writer doesn't know what that purpose is, the reader will not know either.

Each body paragraph of the letter should have a clear point—one that falls under the thematic umbrella presented in the opening paragraph. Each body paragraph should also contain necessary elaboration and details, but it should not go on endlessly. White space is popular with readers, who appreciate a paragraph break between ideas.

The language throughout the letter should be easy to understand. Writers too often rely on business jargon and don't recognize the power of natural language and vocabulary.

Finally, proofreading matters! I wish more letter writers would print out their letters and read them aloud before sending them. They would find so many more mistakes that way.

9

Thank you very much for listening to my concerns. I have enclosed a copy of my all-time favorite letter for your files. I hope you enjoy it as much as I did.

Sincerely,

Jack Brown

Jack Brown
VP, Business Development

Enclosure

Sample Business Letter

9.2 Presentation Slides as Textual Assaults

For PowerPoint or other presentation slides, more is not better. In fact, as much as you can possibly avoid it, do not fill slides with text.

Many slides are crowded with text so dense you cannot read it. They may have sub-bullets or even sub-bullets of sub-bullets. No one likes to read bullets and sub-bullets recreationally. You have probably never heard anyone say, "Great, I have some free time this weekend! I'm going to sit in the backyard and read some bulleted lists to relax!"

Don't do this:

Text-Filled Slide

Unfortunately, many organizations now expect oral presentations to be accompanied by slides full of bullets, and there may not be much you can do to override standard templates used for presentations at your company. However, as much as your situation permits, think of slides as a place *not* to heap giant piles of text. Think about visual representations instead—or go slideless. History is full of examples of effective slideless presentations.

9.3 Thank-You Notes Move Mountains

A sincere note expressing appreciation for an interview or a favor can move mountains, develop professional relationships, or earn you business. Appreciating people for what they do is a valuable human skill.

Emailed thank-you notes are fine, but for a personal touch, consider writing something by hand. You can even buy nice stamps thematically linked to your business interests! Because almost no one sends them anymore, a handwritten, hand-addressed card really stands out these days.

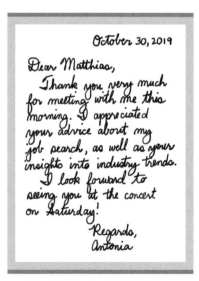

Handwritten Thank-You Note

The example here uses cursive, but feel free to print if your handwriting is messy.

9.4 Instant Messaging: No Excuse for Bad Writing

If you use texting or instant messaging at work, stay as close as you can to your usual standards of writing professionalism in what you send. Whether you type the messages quickly or not, they will endure a lot longer than the amount of time you put into composing them. What you message represents you in your absence.

9.5 Common Weaknesses in Proposals

When companies and other organizations send out requests for proposals (RFPs), they often ask for a particular combination of information in a particular order.

Whatever the format, here are several common mistakes people make:

1. They instinctively feel longer is better. They may not even realize they feel longer is better, but you would know it if you weighed their proposals.

9

2. They talk about themselves too much rather than focusing on the needs of the client.

3. They copy large swaths of previous proposals. They don't revisit and edit this recycled text, so it feels irrelevant or at best generic when the recipient reads it.

4. There is too much repetition. For example, one RFP may call for individual bios in a separate section. The proposal writer may paste those in without realizing he has already included bios in the corporate overview from a previous proposal. The bios show up twice, the proposal is bigger, and the proposal writer feels happy about how much it weighs.

5. The proposal doesn't respond to the specific features of the RFP. A good proposal is in part a listening task.

People are in a rush to meet proposal deadlines. Maybe they can't always produce the ideal proposal in the time that they have. But watching for these common shortcomings can increase the likelihood that a proposal you spend time on results in business.

9.6 The Template Trap

If you repeatedly send out emails or other documents containing similar or identical content, you may find it convenient to automate the process by creating some templates.

If you do use templates and you are in the habit of customizing them for individual recipients, be very, very careful. Templates for letters and other communications can save time, but they can also be the source of embarrassing errors.

For example, if a client asks for some specialized information and the writer edits a portion of the usual template, the edits may cause unanticipated problems. These might include typographical errors, an awkward redundancy in content or word choice, or even an outright conflict of information if the writer forgets to make corresponding changes in another, related section.

In some cases, it may be easier and safer to compose from scratch.

9

Chapter 10

The Art of the Sentence

Much of the life and energy of a piece of writing comes from good sentence structure. Poor sentence structure can tire, bore, or confuse the audience. Excellent sentence structure makes your ideas clearer and more fun to read.

10.1 Neverending Sentences

Don't overwhelm your reader with long, tangled sentences. Making your sentences really long does not mean you are writing less. All the conjunctions you have to insert to keep that sentence going are probably adding to your word count.

In addition, by overusing convoluted sentences, writers obscure their ideas behind complex syntax. Busy professionals simply do not want to reread difficult sentences to try to figure out what the writer meant.

One important way to enliven a piece of writing is to vary the length and structure of your sentences. Try reading aloud something you have written. Listen to the rhythm and flow of the sentences.

Is there interest and variety? Or do you notice a repetitive drone? If the latter is the case, you may be in a sentence-structure rut! Try mixing things up a bit. Vary sentence length. Vary the way you combine ideas.

10.2 Sentence Structure Basics

Sentences consist of one or more clauses. A clause is a group of grammatically related words that includes a subject and a predicate.

A subject is a noun or pronoun that performs the action in a clause or that the clause is about.

> The **physician** called the lab.
>
> The **restaurant** had no tables available.
>
> The **CFO** will announce first-quarter results today.

A predicate consists of one or more verbs and accompanying modifiers.

> **Subject** • *Predicate*
>
> The **attorney** *worked all night on her speech.*
>
> Greg's previous **manager** *accepted a position at a competing firm.*
>
> **Sue** and **Ramón** *have submitted an impressive proposal.*

10

The third example above contains a compound subject consisting of two proper nouns (in other words, names). In addition, all three of the preceding examples are independent clauses. That means they are clauses that can stand alone as sentences.

A second clause type is called dependent, meaning it cannot stand alone. A dependent clause—also known as a subordinate clause—begins with a subordinating conjunction. There are dozens of subordinating conjunctions; below is a representative sample.

after	since
although	so that
as	unless
as if	until
because	when
before	whenever
even though	whereas
if	while

In each of the following dependent clauses, the subordinating conjunction launches the clause, which also includes a subject and predicate.

Subordinating Conjunction • **Subject** • *Predicate*

because **he** *forgot his umbrella*

when **Ms. Richards** *called me*

until the **president** *arrives*

To turn the dependent clauses above into independent clauses, simply remove the subordinating conjunction:

He forgot his umbrella.
Ms. Richards called me.
The president arrives.

In their sentences, good writers use a variety of structures: single independent clauses, multiple independent clauses, and a combination of dependent and independent clauses.

10.3 Sentence Variety

Variety adds interest. A simple, punchy idea might be best expressed with a simple sentence structure. A more complicated idea may justify a longer, more complex sentence structure. A mixture of sentence types can make the act of reading your writing a more pleasurable and productive experience for your audience.

Don't avoid a whole category of combining words simply because you don't know how to punctuate them; you will end up relying on too few sentence strategies, and your writing will be less varied and interesting.

This section covers some common sentence types and considers the stylistic consequences of overusing certain structures—or of avoiding them altogether.

Consider the following ideas:

Revenues were plummeting we decided to close two branches.

That group of words contains two clauses—both independent—with no punctuation or combining word to link them. This is a classic example of a run-on sentence: two independent clauses joined together with nothing but air.

The way you link ideas such as those contained in the run-on above has everything to do with sentence style and readability. Below are the main options for punctuating and/or combining these ideas, with commentary on the stylistic nuances of each.

Version 1. Period

Revenues were plummeting. We decided to close two branches.

Although using occasional very short sentences can be a powerful writing technique, these two short sentences sound a bit choppy next to each other.

Version 2. Semicolon

Revenues were plummeting; we decided to
close two branches.

Here the two independent clauses are combined with a semicolon. How does this version differ from Version 1? Well, punctuation marks are like the traffic signals of writing. You could associate the comma with a rolling stop at a stop sign, a semicolon with a quick (but fully legal!) stop at the same sign, and a period with a brief wait at a red light.

Linked with a semicolon, these two clauses read more quickly than they did when separated by a period. Some people, unfortunately, are semicolon-phobic; they never use semicolons, largely because they don't know how. While there is no minimum daily requirement for the semicolon, any time you eliminate one entire sentence-combining method because you are uncomfortable with it, you are limiting your stylistic versatility.

Below are the criteria that justify semicolon use between two independent clauses:

1. The ideas being linked are closely related.
2. When you read the sentence aloud, it sounds good; the ideas flow.

10

Version 2 may not be an award-winning sentence, but it sounds acceptable. Whether it works in a given document would depend in part on the surrounding sentences and how they are structured.

Version 3. Coordinating Conjunction

Revenues were plummeting, so we decided to close two branches.

Coordinating conjunctions such as *so* combine sentence elements of roughly equal weight. There are seven such conjunctions in all. To remember them, think *fanboys*. Each letter in the memory aid *fanboys* represents the first letter of one of the seven coordinating conjunctions:

for
and
nor
but
or
yet
so

Many businesspeople rely too heavily on coordinating conjunctions as a way of linking ideas.

Coordinating conjunctions are useful—in fact, critically important—words in the English language, but overusing them creates writing problems. Because they link elements of similar weight, when they are overused as clause-combining tools, a piece of writing can start to feel like an unsorted heap of ideas and details, without a sense of hierarchy or a sufficiently sturdy structure. This and that. This so that. This but that. This or that. To add variety to your writing style, be sure to use other idea-combining options, too.

In Version 3 on the preceding page, note the comma before the *so*. If you use a coordinating conjunction to combine two independent clauses, it is standard punctuation to include a comma before the conjunction. One exception could be two very short clauses combined with an *and*. In many other cases, leaving the comma out can confuse readers or at least make it more difficult for them to identify the boundary between two ideas. Don't be stingy about those commas.

Version 4. Conjunctive Adverb

Revenues were plummeting; therefore, we decided to close two branches.

Therefore is an example of a conjunctive adverb—in other words, a conjunction-like adverb. There are

10

many such adverbs, though the following five show up particularly often in business writing:

    therefore
    furthermore
    however
    moreover
    nevertheless

The structure of Version 4 on the preceding page is in some ways similar to Version 3, but there are stylistic differences that people who are, ahem, conjunctive adverb addicts should heed. Conjunctive adverb addiction is particularly common in the consulting, legal, academic, and government sectors, but it can be found in virtually every industry.

The overuse of conjunctive adverbs creates a ponderous, heavy writing style. There are two main reasons for that. First, many conjunctive adverbs are on the formal end of the style spectrum. Also, if you look at Version 4, you will see that there are two breaks in the middle of the sentence: a significant break associated with the semicolon, followed by a fairly formal polysyllabic word (the conjunctive adverb), and then another break associated with the comma.

In isolation, in moderation, there's nothing wrong with a structure like that. It's completely appropriate for this content and for this sentence.

Imagine, though, a document in which the writer repeatedly uses this structure to combine clauses. It's a slower structure, with more stops and starts, and more attention drawn to the intersection between ideas, than you see in Version 3. It's like Los Angeles traffic.

Version 5. Subordinating Conjunction

5a. Because revenues were plummeting, we decided to close two branches.

5b. We decided to close two branches because revenues were plummeting.

Versions 5a and 5b illustrate the use of the subordinating conjunction *because* to combine ideas. In 5a, the subordinating conjunction appears at the beginning, thus turning that first clause into a dependent clause, which is then followed by an independent clause (*we decided to close two branches*). In 5b, the sentence begins with an independent clause that is then followed by a dependent clause.

Either sentence is fine. If you are concerned about beginning a sentence with *because*, don't be. Instead, read 12.1 in the chapter on writing myths.

Beginning with *because* creates suspense. The reader arrives at the comma after *plummeting* and is curious. The reader is tempted to read through to the end to get resolution.

10

A mixture of sentence types is exciting and shows writing confidence. If you have fallen into a sentence-structure rut, now is your chance to try new things, to add punch and variety to your words.

10.4 Comma Splices: Beware!

It is common to see two independent clauses joined by a single lonely comma, like this:

> They were stealing pants daily, we had to fire them.

The sentence above is called a *comma splice.* Avoid it in workplace writing. The comma is too frail, too delicate a piece of punctuation, to hold apart two independent clauses without the additional help of some kind of combining word.

Try this:

> They were stealing pants daily, so we had to fire them.

Problem solved!

In business writing, where you can put a period you can virtually never put a comma. If you do, you will in most cases create a comma splice.

10.5 Problematic Passive Voice

Perhaps you have been told before not to use passive voice. Passive voice abounds in business writing. The idea, though, is not to eliminate passive voice entirely; rather, you should avoid excessive or unjustified use of passive voice.

Defining Passive Voice

To reduce passive voice, one must first be able to identify it. The sentence below offers a classic example:

> The results were analyzed by the executive committee.

What makes this sentence passive? Look for the following characteristics:

1. The grammatical subject—*results*, in this example—receives the action of the verb. The results don't do anything; rather, something is done to them.
2. The verbs include the following:
   a) a form of the verb *to be* (*were*, in this example). Besides *were*, other forms of *to be* are as follows: *am*, *is*, *are*, *was*, *be*, *been*, and *being*.
   b) a past participle (here, the word *analyzed*)

10

In case the past participle is a hazy memory (or no memory at all!), here's a way you can bring it to mind: it is the form of a verb that would fit in the blank in *I have _____*.

For regular verbs, the past participle is identical to the past tense (*I have **moved*** vs. *I **moved**, I have **finished*** vs. *I **finished***, etc.). For irregular verbs, the past participle and past tense tend to differ. For instance, the past participle of *to drive* is *driven* (as in *I have driven*), whereas the past tense is *drove*.

If the entity performing the action is included in the sentence, it typically follows the verbs and appears as part of a prepositional phrase—in the example above, *by the executive committee*.

A sentence can contain passive voice without including this information, though. Deleting *by the executive committee* from the sample sentence does not eliminate the passive voice. The following is still a passive construction:

The results were analyzed.

As you look for passive voice, keep in mind that a form of the verb *to be* does not automatically signal a passive construction. For example, how many of the following three sentences contain passive voice?

1. The meeting was not productive for me.
2. The meeting was led by Edna.
3. The meeting was boring the attendees.

In fact, only the second sentence contains passive voice. In the first sentence, *productive* is an adjective, not a past participle. In the third sentence, *boring* is not a past participle either. (Remember, it can't fit in the following blank: *I have* _____.) In addition, the subject of the sentence—*meeting*—is performing the action, namely, boring the attendees. Sentence 3 is actually an example of what is known as active voice, discussed below.

Reducing Passive Voice

In many passive-voice constructions, the writer would be better off rewriting the sentence using active voice. Compare these two versions:

Passive Voice

The results were analyzed by the executive committee.

10

Active Voice

The executive committee analyzed the results.

Active voice is usually preferable to passive voice. It is more direct, and the reader learns first who or what performed the action, then what the action was, and finally who or what was acted upon. That order of information slides smoothly into the brain.

Also, replacing passive with active voice often reduces the number of words by two. We do not need to be too stingy about word count, but adding words in order to be less direct is not a good goal. You need a better reason to justify passive voice.

Watch out for passive-voice constructions such as the following, which appear frequently in business documents:

- it is/was/has been recommended that
- it was/has been decided that
- it was/has been noted that
- it was/has been observed that

In many cases, these phrases are fillers and can simply be eliminated, often with little or no rewriting of the remainder of the sentences that contain them. Compare the original and revised versions of the following sentences (passive voice is italicized):

Original

It was decided that we need to shut down our Oregon plant.

Improved

Unfortunately, we need to shut down our Oregon plant.

* * *

Original

It has been noted that employees have been using their corporate email accounts to send personal messages.

Improved

Employees have been using their corporate email accounts to send personal messages.

* * *

Original

It has been observed that the employee break room is unacceptably messy by the end of the day.

Improved

The employee break room is unacceptably messy by the end of the day.

10

Acceptable Passive Voice

Nonetheless, passive voice is sometimes acceptable, even preferable. For example, it is appropriate in the following cases:

1. when the entity performing the action is unknown

Suppose your dog comes home one night with a cut on her leg, and you don't know the cause of the injury. When you go into work the next day, you tell your assistant, "My dog was injured last night." If you don't know how your dog was injured, it is hard to construct a reasonable active-voice version of this sentence. You would have to say something silly like, "Someone or something injured my dog last night."

2. when the emphasis is properly on the entity receiving the action

For example, you might complain to the head of the marketing department, "Our website hasn't been updated in nearly six months." Here, passive voice emphasizes the fact that your website isn't current. Now, if you wanted to assign blame for this problem, you might instinctively choose active voice instead: "You haven't updated our website in nearly six months!"

10.6 Excessive Use of Prepositional Phrases

Some writers overuse prepositional phrases, repeatedly stringing together four, five, or even more in a row.

This habit is responsible for some of the monster sentences you see in reports and other business documents.

A prepositional phrase consists of two parts: (1) a preposition and (2) the object of the preposition, which is a noun or pronoun, accompanied by any modifiers. Following are some examples of prepositional phrases:

Preposition • **Object**
in the **office**
under the **rug**
over my **head**
during Nathan's **meeting**
before the **interview**

Overusers of prepositional phrases are often motivated by the desire to convey a lot of information in a single sentence, but the result can be a meandering sentence structure that is difficult to follow. Try reading the following sentence aloud (prepositional phrases are indicated with parentheses):

10

The first half (of the new book) (by Roberta Durang) (about the early history) (of XYZ Corporation), one (of the first high-tech companies) (in Texas), includes some remarkable stories (of industry-transforming technological innovation).

Now read aloud this revised version, which breaks the original sentence into two:

> XYZ Corporation was one (of the first high-tech companies) (in Texas). (In her new book) (on the company's early history), writer Roberta Durang tells some remarkable stories (of industry-transforming technological innovation).

The new version is much easier to follow. Dividing the original sentence improves readability, as does reducing the number of consecutive prepositional phrases. In addition, even though the revised example contains two sentences, it is shorter by two words than the original. Increasing the number of sentences can often actually help you reduce the overall number of words!

Chapter 11

Word Choice and Writing Dynamism

When you write for business, try to use words you know well, are in control of, and can imagine yourself actually saying out loud in conversation with another human being. To write powerfully, select your words with care. Careful word choice supports lively, engaging writing.

11.1 Wordiness: Too Much Is Too Much

Wordiness shows a lack of respect for the reader's time. Everyone knows how annoying it is to be sent unnecessarily long documents. Yet millions of people who hate reading unnecessarily long documents persist in sending them.

Stop the madness.

Wordiness also obscures the writer's ideas. It frequently signals a lack of substance. That's not a good signal to send out. A confident, authoritative writer has no need for extra words. Take the time to edit out unnecessary language. If a word doesn't pull its weight, dump it!

11.2 Ornate Language and Faux Fanciness

Related to wordiness is the tendency to use unnaturally ornate expressions in an effort to dress up a piece of writing. Why write *is cognizant of* when you can substitute *is aware of* or *knows about*? Why write *due to the fact that* when *because* will do?

> Bruno is cognizant of the change to the meeting date due to the fact that the room is no longer available.

Ugh. Don't do that to your readers!

Straightforward, efficient language will draw less attention to itself and keep readers' attention on your writing. It will also be easier on their email-inundated brains. They will appreciate you.

11.3 Jargon and Business Buzzwords

Various professions have their own specialized vocabulary, known as *jargon*. Lawyers, computer programmers, physicians, and many other professionals regularly use words that are familiar to their colleagues but mysterious to people in other disciplines.

If you are a biochemist writing for other biochemists, it would be natural and appropriate to refer to *organelles*, *bioassays*, or even *colloidal semiconductor nanocrystals*. If you are a specialist writing for a lay audience, you should minimize specialized jargon, define essential terms, and explain concepts so that a non-specialist can understand them.

In addition to profession-specific jargon, there is a large stockpile of business jargon used across industries. Examples include:

actionable

bandwidth

best of breed

best practices

buy-in

core competencies

deep dive

drill down

enterprise-wide

incent/incentivize/disincent

low-hanging fruit

mission-critical

move the needle

operationalize

optimize

proactive

space

synergy/synergies/synergize

value add

value-added

various abbreviations, particularly those that
aren't widely known

Most of the terms included on this list are so widely used that you may be surprised to see them here. (If you don't recognize them, even better!)

Imagine you are reading a memo on business strategy in which the writer uses these terms prolifically.

We need to incentivize our employees
enterprise-wide to develop core competencies
and best practices proactively, thus
operationalizing our synergies and ensuring
value adds for all of our clients.

Would you understand what that meant? Would the writer know? Probably not. This type of business jargon, however, can be found in the mission statements of more than a few companies.

Abbreviations are a final type of jargon plaguing business documents. The problem arises when people overuse abbreviations that aren't familiar to others. *FBI* and *IRS* are almost universally known, but

11

organizations often use dozens and dozens of obscure abbreviations. They are popular in business writing because they save space—and perhaps, in some cases, because they sound technical and intimidating. Once you learn them, you have special insider status!

Abbreviations are usually a convenience to the writer rather than to the reader. They save typing time (though how much time can they really save?). When overused, abbreviations can confuse and frustrate the audience. Writing etiquette requires that you put the reader's comfort and convenience before any desire you may have to reduce keystrokes.

This is a practice many people already know: write out the first reference in full, followed by the abbreviation in parentheses, as in this example:

The second chapter discusses collateralized loan obligations (CLOs).

Then, for subsequent references, use only the abbreviation.

The mistake people often make is to interpret this standard practice as an invitation to use as many abbreviations as they can. Ask yourself whether you need to use the shortened forms at all. After all, just because ice cream is in the freezer does not mean we need to eat it.

Would it be easier on your reader if you skipped the abbreviations? Do the abbreviations make their lives harder?

If a term with an abbreviation is used only a few times in a document, if the abbreviation is not well-known, and if the reader doesn't need to know it, just skip it. For example, if you use the term *asset-backed security* only three times in a 10-page document, there is in most cases no need to use *ABS* at all.

If you write a 20-page report with 15 abbreviations and you absolutely cannot pare them back, then consider adding a glossary at the end that explains each of them in alphabetical order.

11.4 Clichés and Trite Language

Trite language is language that has become stale through overuse. For example, clichés—trite expressions or sayings—are victims of their own popularity. If, at a meeting, you tell your colleague, "It is what it is," you are using a cliché to express your point.

Clichés have achieved a state of dull predictability. Avoid them. Other examples include:

11

off the radar screen

on the radar screen

get our ducks in a row

on a going-forward basis

think outside the box

stay ahead of the curve

drop the ball

Clichés act as a kind of verbal sedative: they dramatically reduce the likelihood that the reader will heed your message. If you want your reader to pay attention to your words, use fresh, original language. Doing so will support the impression that you also have fresh, original ideas.

11.5 Don't Write Like a Business Robot

Business correspondence often contains unnecessarily ornate expressions such as *please find attached* or *pursuant to your request*. Just as these expressions would sound stilted in speech, they sound stilted in emails, letters, and memos. Replace them with more direct, natural language, as illustrated in the table below.

Ornate Expression	More Natural Alternative
please find attached attached please find	I have attached *or* attached is
please find enclosed enclosed please find	I have enclosed *or* enclosed is
please be advised that	(nothing) *or* please note that
per your request as per your request pursuant to your request	as you requested
per our conversation as per our conversation	as we discussed

Eliminating problematic phrases can dramatically improve your writing style. Consider the effect of a few simple word-choice substitutions in the following pairs of sentences.

Unnecessarily Ornate	Revised
Pursuant to your request, please find attached the status report.	As you requested, I have attached the status report.
Please be advised that the meeting will begin at 4:00 instead of 3:30.	The meeting will begin at 4:00 instead of 3:30.
As per our conversation, I have asked Barbara to research the new location.	As we discussed, I have asked Barbara to research the new location.

11

Here is another example of a common stock sentence in email:

> Please feel free to call or email me with any
> comments, questions, or suggestions.

The sentence is not disastrous, but it is wordy. The problem is that some people will use the identical sentence in almost every email, sometimes even embedding the sentence into their signature file to save time. If the emailer puts the same sentence in every email, what is the effect?

A bad one. The etiquette benefits erode fast, as it is clear the emailer is on autopilot and is not actually thinking about what he is writing.

The idea behind such a sentence is a good one, but mix it up! Pare it down! Exclude it from emails where it isn't relevant!

Here are variations that could work in different email contexts:

> I would be glad to answer any questions.
>
> Please feel free to contact me with any
> comments or questions.
>
> Please call or email me with any questions.

Please let me know if you have any questions.

You are welcome to call any time with questions or suggestions.

Most writing can't be automated. If you try to automate it, you risk sounding inauthentic. Even subtle variations make an enormous difference to the quality of your word choice and your communications.

11.6 Precision Has Business Value

Suppose you are a managing director reading an annual performance review that one of your vice presidents wrote about an employee, Tina, in your department. You encounter the following sentence, which appears in the review without elaboration:

Tina does consistently sloppy work.

What does *sloppy* mean? Does Tina not fact-check? Does she fail to proofread? Is she messy?
This is better:

Tina's proposals consistently contain mathematical and other factual errors.

Now we—and Tina's managing director, and Tina herself—can understand what the problem is. Perhaps Tina will have a chance to improve the quality of her proposals, enhance her overall performance, and contribute more to the company. This example illustrates how good writing can be good business.

It is also a kindness to make clear what you mean to people who are vulnerable to your assessments.

Besides specificity, precise writing requires the right word for the right occasion. Don't try to be fancy and make a mistake in the process! Here is a sentence where that has happened:

> During the next year, we intend to accelerate our market share in the financial services sector.

The writer has misused *accelerate*, which involves increasing the speed of something. Since one can't increase the speed of market share, this is the wrong word. In this case, the more mundane—and more accurate—*increase* would be a good substitute. Use words that will help people understand you more, not less.

11.7 Excessive Use of Linking Verbs

In business writing, vigorous, energetic language is useful! One of the best ways to increase the vigor of your writing is to avoid the excessive use of linking verbs, which are verbs that describe a state of being.

The most common linking verb is *to be*, whose basic forms are as follows: *am, is, are, was, were, be, been*, and *being*.

Other examples of linking verbs include *appear, feel, look, seem, sound*, and *smell*. Depending on how they are used, most of these additional examples can sometimes also be action verbs, which, as the name indicates, describe action.

For instance, in the following sentence, *appeared* is a linking verb because it describes a state of being.

The manager appeared tired.

But in this next sentence, *appeared* is an action verb because it describes an occurrence; something happens in the sentence.

The manager appeared in the doorway.

Other examples of action verbs include *repair, arrive, audit, testify, rotate*, and *brainstorm*. These, as well as most other action verbs, can't double as linking verbs.

When you write, you will naturally need to use both linking and action verbs; both verb types play a critical role in the English language. However, the overuse of linking verbs can sometimes leave a piece of writing flat. Where possible, don't just tell what something is; tell what it does.

Consider the following simple sentence:

Mark is tall.

In this example, the linking verb *is* describes a state of being. In the example below, however, a similar concept is expressed with an action verb, *towers.*

Mark towers over his colleagues.

The two sentences show how the use of an action verb can enliven a sentence. The point is not that the sentence *Mark is tall* is deficient; in fact, depending on the context, it could work perfectly well. However, the choice between *is* and a more active alternative becomes important when linking verbs appear in abundance in a piece of writing.

Below are two versions of a paragraph from a business letter (key verbs are boldfaced):

Version 1

There **are** three factors influencing my decision to end partnership discussions with you. First, you **are** not knowledgeable about industry regulations. Second, you **are** often several days late in returning my phone calls. Third—and most important—you **are** not willing to sign an agreement limiting my liability in case the business **is** unsuccessful.

Version 2

Three factors **caused** me to end partnership discussions with you. First, you do not **know** the industry regulations. Second, you often **take** several days to return my phone calls. Third—and most important—you have **refused** to sign an agreement limiting my liability in case the business **fails**.

The language in both versions is standard and fairly basic—nothing out of the ordinary. But in the second version, action verbs replaced each instance of *is* or *are* from the first. The second version is crisper and more dynamic. Where there is overreliance on linking verbs, replacing just a few of them can transform a page of writing. Just make sure you don't twist your sentences into pretzels trying to avoid a simple *is*. The verb *to be* is still our friend.

A final technical note: in seeking out linking verbs, don't get mistakenly distracted by sentences such as the following.

11

Jen is rewriting the letter.

Rob and Pat are editing the report.

In both of these cases, the main verbs are the action verbs—*rewriting* and *editing*, respectively—and the forms of *to be* simply act as helping verbs. They help by showing, in combination with the *-ing* endings on the main verbs, that Jen is in the midst of rewriting, while Rob and Pat are in the midst of editing. (An industrious bunch!) These sentences do not contain linking verbs and are therefore not relevant for this discussion.

Chapter 12

Writing Myths

Many people base a life's worth of writing decisions on something they *think* they remember a teacher once told them. Prohibitions have a powerful hold on youthful imaginations, but memory is imperfect, teachers are imperfect, our understanding of language advances, and it is important that we remain open to new ideas and information throughout our lives.

This chapter details writing myths that hobble writers in professional contexts. Do not allow these myths to prevent you from saying what you need to say.

12.1 Myth #1. Don't begin a sentence with *because*.

This one is first for a reason. Prejudice against the earnest, hardworking word *because* is widespread—and it is unjustified!

The prejudice against *because* as a sentence starter leads to numerous writing problems, as professionals go through all sorts of language contortions to avoid what is a perfectly good sentence structure. In avoiding it unnecessarily, they impoverish their writing style, because *because* is a perfectly good word and some of the substitutes are awful.

> Because he embezzled millions of dollars, he spent the rest of his life in jail.

Many people will automatically flip these two clauses to eliminate the starting *because*:

> He spent the rest of his life in jail because he embezzled millions of dollars.

But flipping the clauses sucks much of the life and energy from the sentence.

Other people will meticulously cross out *because* and replace it with *due to the fact that*.

> Due to the fact that he embezzled millions of dollars, he spent the rest of his life in jail.

This structure is wordy, awkward, and inherently inferior to the version beginning with *because*.

For those who remain uncomfortable with the idea of beginning with *because*: if you have spent your whole life avoiding *because* at the beginnings of sentences, but have at the same time been starting

12

sentences with *if*, or *when*, or *while*, you have been guilty of grammatical hypocrisy!

The following four sentences are structurally identical; each starts with a dependent clause and concludes with an independent clause:

> Because her train was delayed, Sue missed the meeting.
>
> If her train is delayed, Sue will catch a cab.
>
> When her train is delayed, Sue catches a cab.
>
> While Sue was waiting for her train, she called one of her colleagues.

There is nothing wrong with any of them. So why do so many teachers tell students not to begin sentences with *because*? After all, this writing "rule" was—and is—bad advice, ignored by good writers everywhere.

Presumably, some teachers believe this prohibition to be legitimate, but others may view it as a practical means to an end, without necessarily believing it to be a requirement for good grammar. Consider, after all, the favorite question of every small child: "Why?" The answer, inevitably, begins with *because*. Left to their own devices, many children will write things like the following:

I like chocolate bunnies. Because they taste
good.

The problem with the second piece—*because they taste good*—is not that it begins with *because*, but that it is a fragment, a mere piece of a sentence.

Across the US, anti-*because* superstition keeps adults from expressing their ideas as directly and powerfully as they might. In the meantime, professional writers don't give this matter a second thought. When they need that starting *because*, they grab it.

Heed the pros.

12.2 Myth #2. Don't begin a sentence with *and* or *but*.

Regardless of what you may have been told in school, you can find plenty of sentences beginning with *and* and *but* in professional writing. It is a common technique in more playful writing such as marketing and advertising copy. Book writers do it; journalists do it, too.

However, avoiding sentences that begin with *and* or *but* isn't going to create problems for people writing in a business context. You don't *need* to do it, and unless you are confident you already have an

12

advanced sense of style and sentence rhythm, you might want to skip it.

If you are interested in incorporating such a sentence into your writing, pay attention, when you read the news, to how skilled journalists use this technique in their own writing. Whether you decide to use it yourself or not, it will at least be helpful to know that it is not a mistake when you see it.

12.3 Myth #3. Don't end a sentence with a preposition.

Do you want to have friends? Do you want to be invited to parties? If you go around saying "That is the restaurant at which I'd like to eat" instead of "That's the restaurant I'd like to eat at," no one will ever invite you to eat at *any* restaurant.

This myth about prepositions was debunked ages ago. It was based on a false application of Latin grammar to English grammar. The languages are different. Other Germanic languages end with prepositions all the time, and their speakers don't freak out.

There are limitations, however. Don't do this:

That's the book I just finished reading the first half of.

That's awkward. Don't do that in writing. But it is often fine to end a sentence with a preposition. Make sure your sentence sounds natural and you are set.

12.4 Myth #4. Don't split an infinitive.

Here are three examples of infinitives:

> to win
>
> to write
>
> to triple

Some of us were taught as children that you should never put a word (usually an adverb) between the *to* in the infinitive and the rest of the verb.

It is not true. The split-infinitive ban is in the grammar dustbin, but not everyone has heard the news yet. Or cares, because they learned it in eighth grade and "That teacher was a saint!"

What is still true is that there is no need to go out of your way to split infinitives, especially if you are trying to put a whole bunch of things between the *to* and the rest of the verb, as in:

> We need **to** methodically, thoroughly, and carefully **analyze** the book.

12

That doesn't sound good, it's wordy, and it's just not necessary.

This next sentence can't be unsplit, however, and shouldn't be.

> You need **to** more than **double** your billable
> hours.

12.5 Myth #5. Never use *I think, I feel, I hope.*

Do not attach caveats and qualifiers to all your statements. It sounds weak and wishy-washy to qualify everything you say. But it is dishonest to say something is true when you don't actually know it's true.

If you are not sure about an assertion, by all means preface it with *I believe* or an equivalent. The following two sentences are very different, and only one is reasonable.

> We will double our revenues this quarter.
> I believe we will double our revenues this
> quarter.

We are not fortunetellers, and one can't always be certain of outcomes.

Chapter 13

Editing Tips

Careful editing can turn a weak document into a powerful piece of writing. Editing takes place on many levels. It can range from a quick review of a short email message to an exhaustive, and possibly exhausting, revision process involving many document drafts with contributions from multiple writers.

With a systematic approach to editing, you can fix organizational flaws, improve sentence structure and word choice, and avoid common proofreading mistakes. In this chapter you will find a series of tips for a healthy editorial philosophy. Some apply only to longer documents; most apply to all.

13.1 Check Your Eyesight

If you can't properly see what's on your screen, it will be harder to edit, so here are two questions for you:

1. Do you have perfect vision or, alternatively, reading glasses that perfect your vision when you put them on?
2. Are your computer settings (lighting, font size, resolution, etc.) the best they can possibly be?

If you can't answer yes to both, take action! You deserve to be comfortable, and good editing demands clear-sightedness.

13.2 The Psychology of Writing

It is natural to suffer during the writing process. Editing is part of that process, and it involves careful thought and hard work; it isn't always easy. In fact, it quite regularly isn't!

If you find you are suffering mightily through the revision process, keep in mind that people all over the world are experiencing similar or identical feelings this very minute—while editing! You are not alone! Revising won't always be painful, but suffering may well mean you're doing something right. Don't think it's stressful just because you personally haven't figured out the key to it.

In addition, don't feel bad if you wind up with a lot of drafts. Professional writers often go through many, many drafts of a document, especially if it is a longer document, before they feel satisfied with it.

The goal is not to get a piece of writing perfect the first or second time. Rather, the goal is to use whatever combination of writing and editing strategies works best for you personally—with your unique combination of strengths, weaknesses, and

13

idiosyncrasies—to ensure you get the outcome you want. You won't have time to write multiple drafts of every email, but the point is, you should never burden yourself with the goal of instant perfection.

Lastly, do not fetishize speed. Some people are concerned that they are too slow. They look around and see people sending five email messages, or writing three reports, in the time that it takes them to write one. Speeding up the writing and editing process is nice, but it is rarely the top priority.

After all, many of the people who are shipping out writing as fast as they can type should stop doing that immediately. The very best writers tend to compose and edit with care. Unless you aren't getting your work done, don't measure your speed against the speed of others.

The grass on the other side often isn't even green.

13.3 Outlining as an Organization Check

People are often taught to create outlines before they begin writing. Fewer people are familiar with outlining as an editing technique that can help them once they have finished a draft, but it can be a tremendously powerful tool.

To create an informal post-draft outline, consider printing your document with wide margins so you can write in them. Underline the thesis or main idea of your document. If you can't find a thesis, rewrite until you have one.

Then read through the entire document, jotting in the margin each new topic you come across. Once you have finished, analyze your thesis and margin notes to see whether you can find any structural failings.

Is there needless repetition? Does every paragraph of the body relate to the thesis? Are the ideas presented in a reasonable order?

You can use outlining to help you figure out whether you are accomplishing your organizational goals.

13.4 Process Management

Finish your first draft as far ahead of time as you can. If you spread the revision process out over a longer period, you will have more opportunities to come to your document fresh—and to edit with a clear head. Having 12 separate encounters with a proposal over the course of two weeks is far more valuable than a one-day writing binge, even if the total number of minutes spent on the project is identical.

13

In a longer document, don't try to fix everything at once. It is usually most efficient to edit first for organizational issues and then later for details such as sentence structure, word choice, and grammar. Otherwise you may be fixing verb forms and comma placement in sentences that you will ultimately cut for structural reasons.

Be flexible, though. If you are perplexed about how to fix an organizational problem, try spending a little time editing for something else: tone, wording, passive voice, and so on. Editing for other issues when you are stuck can be a helpful way to get to know your document better and understand its strengths and weaknesses more intimately. Sometimes that greater familiarity will lead to an organizational breakthrough.

If you are confronting a particularly tricky editing problem, leave the document alone for a while. Eat. Return calls. Jog. With a little distance between you and your editing problem, you will be more likely to find a solution once you return to your document, and you will be able to edit more efficiently.

13.5 Reference Materials and Technology Tools

It is common for people to buy dictionaries and other language tools and then leave them unopened on the shelf, or unused online. Reference books aren't helpful unless their owners refer to them. The more you use them, the more you will learn and the more adept you will become at finding the information you need.

Merriam-Webster (m-w.com) and American Heritage (ahdictionary.com) both have excellent dictionary content online for free. If you do a lot of editing, consider investing in a subscription to *The Chicago Manual of Style* (chicagomanualofstyle.org) or seeing if your company might even already have a subscription. You can also buy the physical book, but the index is quite detailed and you may prefer to find what you need using the online edition's search tool.

Professionals are judged on their grammar and spelling. Whether fair or unfair, readers are likely to draw conclusions about larger competence when they see multiple misspellings. The grammar- and spell-checking features of your word-processing software are other tools that can help you find mistakes.

Do not, however, rush through the spell-checking process automatically accepting every spelling suggestion offered to you. You may mean to type this:

The ban was inadequate.

But then you type:

The van was inadequate.

13

Your spell-checker will view this sentence as correct. Help your spell-checker help you.

13.6 Print and Read Your Document

It is often easier to find typographical errors and other writing problems on a printed page than on the computer screen. Although it can feel more efficient to edit electronically, many writers benefit from a combination of online and hardcopy editing.

Reading aloud enables you to hear the rhythm of your writing and thus identify places where the language is awkward or choppy. It also forces you to read more carefully, making you more likely to notice typographical errors or missing words.

Printing and reading aloud in combination is an especially potent combination.

13.7 Editing Teamwork!

When you go to a bookstore and take a book off the shelf, there has typically been a team involved in that book's production. Besides the writer, there might have been multiple editors for multiple versions. There are other team members, too, involved in layout and other features of the publication.

Asking just *one* other person in your office to look at your documents from time to time can provide insight into how your ultimate audience will receive what you've written. A fresh perspective can be extremely helpful.

If you do a lot of writing and editing, perhaps you and a colleague could arrange to review each other's documents on an ongoing basis. Working as a team, you can improve overall document quality together.

This is not for everyone—some people prefer to write on their own—but if you have a colleague who enjoys collaboration in the same way you do, it is a strategy worth considering.

13

Conclusion

We live in an age of writing. When in human history have people written more than they do now? Phone calls of a generation ago are now emails, texts, instant messages, and online posts. Today it is often through the written word that we seek to persuade, educate, clarify needs and intentions, inspire. Younger people write much more, on average, than their parents did.

If you have excellent writing skills, you have a real professional asset. If you improve your writing skills, you can improve your overall job performance and help people work with you more easily. Good writers are useful, and they are valued.

Beware the temptation of ubiquitous technology, however. Some people answer messages as if they were playing a video game. Boom! Splat! Kapow! Efficiency is important, but is it actually efficient to constantly interrupt what one is doing in order to answer a message the moment it arrives?

If you are a compulsive email checker—and if compulsively checking email is not your actual job—consider whether you might be able to cut back on the frequency with which you check your inbox (or other communication media). Depending on the nature of your work, you may not be able to do so, but if you can, you may find your way to a less scattered, more productive workday.

There is no good writing without good thinking—and it is impossible to think clearly about two or three things at the same time. To the extent that you can control the workflow rather than permitting the workflow to control you, your creative thinking and your writing process will be better off.

That in turn will improve the quality of the words you put into the world, and the experience of the people who receive them. Language is power; use it wisely.

About the Author

Ellen Jovin is a co-founder and principal of Syntaxis, a communication skills training firm based in New York City. She has taught business writing, grammar, and email etiquette at companies throughout the United States and in all major industries. Previously she worked as a professional writer specializing in business, finance, and technology. Ellen earned a BA in German studies from Harvard University and an MA in comparative literature from UCLA. She lives in Manhattan with her husband, Brandt Johnson.

About Syntaxis

Syntaxis is a communication skills training firm based in New York City. The company was founded in 1999 by the author of this book, Ellen Jovin, and her husband, Brandt Johnson.

Through workshops and one-on-one coaching, Syntaxis helps people at all stages of their careers, from new hires to CEOs, to communicate with greater clarity, authenticity, and power.

Subject areas include business writing, grammar, email etiquette, editing, presentation skills, executive presence, pitch preparation, and English as a foreign language. All Syntaxis training is delivered by one of the two founders, either Ellen or Brandt. Ellen conducts the training in written communication skills, while Brandt conducts the training in presentation skills and executive presence.

Syntaxis clients include many of the world's leading corporations.

For more information, please visit syntaxis.com.

Index

Other Business Communication Pocket Guides

Essential Grammar for Business: The Foundation of Good Writing by Ellen Jovin

Practical Presentation Skills: Authenticity, Focus & Strength by Brandt Johnson